The MICHIGAN DOGMAN

——WEREWOLVES——
AND OTHER UNKNOWN CANINES ACROSS THE U.S.A.

The
UNEXPLAINED
Presents

The MiCHiGAN DOGMAN

—WEREWOLVES—
AND OTHER UNKNOWN CANINES ACROSS THE U.S.A.

BY LINDA S. GODFREY

UNEXPLAINED
Research Publishing Company
A Division of Unexplained Research LLC

The Michigan Dogman:
Werewolves and Other Unknown Canines Across the U.S.A.
by Linda S. Godfrey

Unexplained Research Publishing Company
A Division of Unexplained Research LLC
P.O. Box 2173, Eau Claire, WI 54702-2173
Email: info@unexplainedresearch.com
www.unexplainedresearch.com

Publisher's Cataloging-in-Publication

Godfrey, Linda S.
　　The Michigan dogman : werewolves and other unknown
　　canines across the U.S.A. / by Linda S. Godfrey.
　　　　p. cm.
　　Includes bibliographical references and index.
　　LCCN 2010935959
　　ISBN-13: 978-0-9798822-6-5
　　ISBN-10: 0-9798822-6-5

　　1. Werewolves--Michigan. 2. Werewolves--United
States. 3. Cryptozoology--United States.　I. Title.

GR830.W4G63 2010　　　　　　398.24'54

All artwork and photos created and copyrighted by the author unless otherwise noted.
Little dog icon: *Mythological and Fantastic Creatures*, Dover Publications, Minneola NY, 2002
Sketches submitted by witnesses: Names withheld
Front cover art: Troy Therrien
Copyeditor: Sarah Szymanski
Cover design: Terry Fisk

DEDICATION

This book is dedicated to all lovers—and mere likers as well—of strange creature fact, fancy and lore.

Table of Contents

Acknowledgements

First thanks go to Chad Lewis and Terry Fisk for their great patience, friendship and belief in this book. I also owe a huge debt of gratitude to the witnesses who contributed their experiences to this growing body of creature lore; it takes time, courage and a generous heart to do so. Much appreciation to my family, as well, for pizza suppers and enduring my long hours glued to my laptop, to the Media Maven Breakfast Association for listening, to Kevin Nelson, Todd Roll, Noah Voss, PC Hodgell, Kim Del Rio, Bart Nunnelly, *The Unknown Creature Spot* crew, Brad Steiger, The *Weird New Jersey* guys, Nick Redfern, Bill Hancock and Derek Grebner for various support and to everyone who has attended a talk or signing, read my blogs, tweeted back, listened to a radio show or watched a program appearance. You are what keep me going.

Introduction

The creature does not languish; it has not retired. That means I may not rest, either. It comes skulking through my emails, prowling in my phone, or holing up inside stamped envelopes posted from Maine. The reports are legion, and sometimes demanding. People see an unidentifiable creature, and they want to know what it is and what it wants. But what they seek most urgently is some logical reason why *they* were chosen to learn that, indeed, unexplained things exist.

The last time I checked, humanity had yet to learn everything there is to know. As a human, therefore—and in the absence of a captured specimen—I don't know everything about this beast. In fact, I know very little that I could cite as fact. Not even after seventeen years of research, expeditions, interviews, reports, the polygraphing of witnesses and much writing of books. There simply is no tangible evidence—aside from a few footprints—that unknown, upright canids walk among us.

That does not mean I lack for theories. Most of them settle somewhere to either slope of the great divide: natural animal or supernatural thing...a cryptozoological beast or, as J.K. Rowling has whimsically put it, a "magizoological"one. For all we know, it could turn out to be something that straddles both categories. Or "it" could be comprised of a variety of phenomena, from misidentified animals to relict species to otherworldly entities we can never hope to capture in physical form unless someone invents a *Ghostbusters* movie-style capture machine. Not holding my breath for that.

What I *do* have is a mountain of encounter reports. Many are from Wisconsin and Michigan, my main theaters of operation, but surprising numbers also come from all parts of the United States and other countries.

My first book, *The Beast of Bray Road* (2003), looked at the incidents I had learned about in the first decade after the initial reports. The second book, *Hunting the American Werewolf* (2006), told of the reports that came to me after *Beast's* publication. In only three years, twice as many witnesses as I covered in *Beast* had come forth. And now, four more years have passed and my accordion file of reports has expanded to bursting.

It helped a great deal that the History Channel's popular *MonsterQuest* show featured *Hunting* as the basis of their "American Werewolf" episode. But most of the people who tell their tales of shock and wonder at meeting a wolf that walks upright still seem reluctant to talk, and are often referred to me by relatives or friends. Others say they simply wish to confess their experience to someone who won't tell them they are crazy. And they are in no danger there. No matter how weird their experience may be, I've almost always heard weirder.

Furry things with bat-wings that dive-bomb old pickup trucks— pint-sized T. rexes scrimmaging through a cornfield near Sheboygan— white canines that vaporize before a witness's astounded eyes—werewolves slumming in the sewers of Minot, North Dakota: heard 'em all and more.

I also receive reports that clearly describe a large primate—Bigfoot, I presume—and the witnesses who get a good look at the heads and legs of these creatures are always very sure which is which. The dogmen feature prominent, pointed ears on top of their heads, muzzles, a much leaner physique, and walk on clawed toe-pads. Other than sharing an upright stance with Bigfoot, the two are as similar as a hyena is to a chimpanzee. And while I cited some Bigfoot sightings in previous books to highlight the fact that often sightings of both canine and primate creatures occur in roughly the same geographical areas, the result was that some people (and TV shows) tended to blend the two. I still may mention BF sightings when pertinent but will not discuss most in detail.

As a side note on the witnesses, I keep their identities private if they wish, using first names or aliases, but I have their original statements and contact information available to my publisher. I don't provide that contact info to anyone else without the witness's permission. I use their own words when possible, but I paraphrase or edit for spelling, punctuation, clarity and brevity as needed—whatever it takes to best tell their tale in a reader-friendly way that is still faithful to the report.

And just as I did in the introduction of *Hunting*, I wish to make it perfectly clear that these are eyewitness reports, which in themselves are not conclusive proof. The evidence for unknown upright canines is mostly anecdotal, save for some photographs of footprints and those witnesses who have passed the tests of the most competent polygraph expert the History Channel could find. (And no, I don't think that any of the wereblob photos presently circulating on the Internet, particularly those of something brown that may or may not be holding a small white dog, are good enough to prove that the manwolf exists.)

These reports may be considered entertainment, food for thought, or an anecdotal database. They do not constitute an excuse for armed expeditions or trespassing on any private property. I do not lead organized "werewolf hunts."

Now that we have that all settled, this one sticking point remains: hundreds of witnesses say that the creature does exist. And mini-T.rexes and manbats aside,

Author interpretation of most witness descriptions of manwolf

these observations of manwolves and dogmen remain surprisingly consistent in both appearance and behavior. Something that stands between five and seven feet tall, covered in shaggy fur ranging from gray to very dark brown, long-snouted, pointy-eared, and able to get around on two or four feet and switch between the modes easily…this is what most people report. Many see the creature holding or eating animal carrion, and although it often bluffs a chase or attack, in almost every case (the one exception being a man in Quebec Province, Canada, who said his hip was grazed by an errant fang) the creature retreats as soon as the witness is either scared senseless or departs the scene.

I would expect far greater variation if people were making up stories.

And I would expect far fewer reports.

Frankly, I would expect that such creatures did not exist at all. But judging by my emails, I am wrong. Something exists, and it looks rather like a werewolf. Readers who wish to know why and how may read on. Everyone else should turn back right now and take the short, straight path—the one that avoids the forest *and* the tall grass—and resume mundane life. Despite what Warren Zevon sang, no werewolf has really ever been seen at Trader Vic's or Starbucks. You'll be safe.

Probably.

PART ONE

The Michigan Dogman

Chapter 1

Dogmanity

It's the question everyone asks me, second only to "what is it?"

"Have you seen the creature yourself?"

Up until the summer of 2006, the answer was always a wistful, "No." Ever since then, it's been an equally wistful, "Partly, perhaps." I still cannot honestly say exactly what it was that ran across a secluded gravel road just north of Reed City, Michigan that steamy July night around 1:00 a.m., but I know that it had gray fur, ran upright and stood at least six feet tall since it blotted out a reflective road sign as it passed.

I was there swatting mosquitoes and surveying thick woods and a small, vacant building with a videographer for History Channel's *MonsterQuest.* The videographer and I were in Michigan to track the Michigan Dog Man, the Beast of Bray Road's upright Michigan cousin. We were filming the segment of *MonsterQuest* titled "American Werewolf," which was based largely on my book, *Hunting the American Werewolf.* Three young people who claimed to have seen two different upright, wolf-like creatures at that spot on several recent occasions accompanied us.

I'll admit we were all a bit nervous. We had staked the place out for several hours, catching yellow eyes blinking at us from the bushes and at one time, hearing what sounded exactly like a very large dog shaking out its fur—a sound no dog owner could fail to identify—no more than thirty feet from the road.

Adding to the eeriness, a motion detector on the building lit periodically when none of us were near it. We trained some large flashlights up and down the little-used road and across the building's front lawn, and we agreed that *something* was circling us, staying just outside the lit areas. Since the witnesses claimed to have seen upright, wolf-like creatures there several other times, they were quite sure they knew what that something was. And it seemed like a good opportunity to finally get photographic proof.

Urban Legend Turns Real

In early June, 2006, I had received an email from Michigan college student John Lyons. He wrote that on the night of June 7, at about 2:30 a.m., he and three male friends had gone to check out an old "church" (actually a school) because they had heard rumors of dogmen in that area. One of the friends, Shawn, had visited the area before and had his own sighting. That night, the three parked in front of the partially rehabbed building, which is surrounded by woods and marsh, then settled back to wait in the darkness.

I had found the case compelling not only because of the recent nature of the sightings, but because the events involved multiple witnesses and at least two individual creatures. In fact, I had the opportunity to interview Lyons by phone only a day after his initial sighting. The following is a slightly edited transcript of the interview I conducted on June 8, the same day he emailed me. His quotes are in response to my questions.

"There were crickets all around," John said, "and all of a sudden they all stopped. I kept on seeing something move over in the woods, kind of a silhouette. I thought it was a deer until we shined the light on it. Must have been six-foot-nine, it was huge, tall! It was a humanoid, I could see below the midsection, could see thighs but not feet. I'm believing it's bipedal. The hair was either dark brown or black, probably dark brown, must have covered most of the body, maybe an inch long. We did see one arm; one of my friends saw it. His arm was longer than human. We were sitting in the car...comparing it to our own bodies.

"We were about fifty feet away. It was behind a tree, in a little wooded area, and it stood half behind the tree and half exposed."

Frightened, the trio decided to leave. They drove away but returned after a few minutes, determined to figure out what they had seen. They were startled when the building's motion light went on, and they heard something moving quickly through the brush.

"My buddy sitting in the back of my hatchback car said, 'What's that?'" wrote John.

"In the tall weeds on the side of the road were two yellow eyes, kind of slanted in a way. It didn't have a long snout like a dog, the snout was narrow. It wasn't human and it wasn't dog. It wasn't flat-faced like a human; all I saw was hair underneath what I presumed to be a jaw, like a cape or mane. From what I saw it was slender in stature, not beefy, I would guess 210-220 pounds. The head reminded me of a canine shape, the kind of triangle-looking head. It was looking straight on at us. It could have had ears but it was too dark to see them…I've seen pictures of Bigfoot but I don't think this was Bigfoot.

"When we saw it in the light when it was standing still (the first time), it looked a little hunched," he added. "I had the distinct feeling this thing wanted to hurt us…I was holding the mag light and I was shaking so bad I actually dropped it. When we left, the eyes were behind the car and the guy looking back thought he saw something go from two to four legs. It went down on all fours and went really fast."

The creature chased the car for a short time the second time they drove away, John told me.

"I'll Put a Bible on What I Just Said"

"It was not a human in a suit or a bear. I'll put a Bible on what I just said…I'm majoring in radiology, so I know enough about the body systems and anatomy to tell about the features. I didn't notice any reproductive organs, there was a lot of hair in that area. I don't think this was (a) paranormal (creature); it was biological, not ghostly.

"I got home and I was so intrigued and freaked out I sat down and Googled 'dog man' and got your web site."

John told me that he was determined to go back for yet another look, and he did so the following week with Shawn and their friend, Aubrey. I received this email from him at 3:57 a.m. on June 15.

"Linda, pardon the French but there is some weird s--- going on here…I cannot describe the depth of how freaked out I am right now."

John said that he, Shawn, and Aubrey had waited for only ten minutes that night before spotting a "light-shaded object in the woods." After a few minutes they shined their mag light at it and estimated it stood about 80 feet from the car.

"This thing was gray and big," John wrote, "unlike my first sighting about a week ago. When I saw it, it was kind of squatting but not really; the closest thing I can relate it to was how an ape sits."

The trio was frightened enough to leave, and as John turned on the ignition, Shawn yelled that the creature had stood up. They drove about half a mile, but when it did not chase them, again they decided to return to make sure they weren't just imagining something. It only took a few minutes before they spotted the same, light colored "object."

"Now the next few things I am going to tell you might not be in exact order," he wrote, "because to be honest I still can't collect all my thoughts."

In essence, John dashed out of the car to get another flashlight from the trunk, and by the time he hopped back in, Shawn and Aubrey had lost sight of the creature. But they began to hear animal noises coming from behind the building. He described them as "not a bark…four or five different pitches…like a pack of dogs fighting over something, but this was not a sound a dog would make. It was far too high-pitched. And almost sequential."

I'm not sure what "almost sequential" means, but the three listened, frozen, for an estimated thirty seconds until the noise ended. It was only another half minute before Aubrey said she heard something outside the car. The building's motion light then went on, and John gunned the engine and drove from the area a final time.

Birthplace of The Legend

Reed City, the Osceola County town also known for its museum dedicated to the famous Christian hymn, "The Old Rugged Cross," lies within easy driving distance of the Lake County berg of Luther, and various sighting spots in Wexford County. These areas are at the heart of Dog Man lore, forever memorialized in the mostly fictional song, "The Legend," by former Traverse City disk jockey, Steve Cook.

Luther was the site of an unexplained animal attack that left claw marks in a house's siding seven feet off the ground, as well as footprints that looked like those of a big dog. Cook wove a few actual incidents like this one together with some old lumber camp lore and tales from other places, then played his spooky recording on April Fool's Day, 1987. He sold CDs of the instant hit to benefit a local animal shelter, and continued to update the song until 2009.

Although Cook was always up-front regarding his original, prankish intentions for "The Legend," he later collaborated with amateur Michigan filmmaker Mike Agrusa to create two videos—showing an unidentifiable quadruped on grainy old Super 8 film—that became known as the Gable Films and tore up Internet forums between 2007 and 2009. The films were exposed as hoaxes on national TV when both men confessed on History Channel's *MonsterQuest* season four finale in 2010. However, the sensational diversion aimed at increasing Cook's CD sales did nothing to disprove other reports from actual witnesses.

Earlier, in 2006, *MonsterQuest* documented the Reed City sightings as supporting evidence for their initial 'American Werewolf' episode. And yet, other than a brief portion of John Lyons' interview, very little of the video shot on that trip made it into the film. A big reason for that was that the new HD camera the crew used somehow added a line of unerasable technical data to every picture frame. Considering how often weird electronics glitches seem to put the kibosh on the documentation of cryptid research, perhaps this shouldn't have seemed surprising.

Something else really did surprise me. My own digital Minolta, which contained images of strange footprints around the schoolhouse, unexplained animal eyes and more, somehow disappeared from the passenger seat of the History Channel's rented van that evening around 1 a.m., after I stopped shooting and placed it there. Who took it? The witnesses were in my view or the cameraman's at all times. Only one car came down the road the whole time we were there, and there were no other dwellings nearby.

It has occurred to me that the witnesses could have arranged to have a companion in a fur suit skulk around the area, and that perhaps this person managed to dart from the bushes, open the door of the van without the videographer or myself taking notice, nab my camera, and then quietly close the door without making even a soft click, but it seems unlikely. We stayed very close to the van. Acoustics were extremely good there, and anyone wearing a fur suit on that hot and muggy night

MonsterQuest **cameraman shoots Mike Agrusa in ghillie suit reenacting his "charge" in the first Gable film**

Painted foam fake intestines created by Mike Agrusa as prop for alleged murder victim Aaron Gable in second Gable film

would have been miserable. Also, no human could duplicate that "wet dog" sound we heard, and human eyes don't shine in the dark.

If true, however, it would also explain the upright "thing" I saw cross the road.

At any rate, all five of us combed the road and the ditches with flashlights for a very long time and never found my camera.

Lacking another explanation, I like to say in jest that the dogman ate my camera. If so, I hope the beast found it indigestible. Having no proof for that scenario, however, I continue to examine all available evidence on this entire cluster of sightings. One factor that argues slightly against the case's validity is the fact that all the witnesses knew each other—a situation that always makes it possible they cooked up the story ahead of time.

With that in mind early on, I interviewed John's friend, Shawn, back in June, 2006. Shawn claimed to have seen the creature a few years earlier with another friend. They were driving by the building one night, he said, when they noticed movement and then saw the yellow eyes.

"It was standing up on two legs, and it was off in the woods at the tree line about 50 feet back," he said. And then it chased their car.

"We were just—we wanted to get the hell out of there. We flew into his dad's driveway. We weren't drinking or nothing; both of us saw it. After that we went once every four months, and we used to go inside the church. One day there was a dead owl spread out inside the door. There was a handprint burned into the wall."

When the *MonsterQuest* crew visited Michigan in 2009 to tape the show's finale, they asked the Reed City witnesses to appear on the episode. John and Shawn both stuck by their stories, but neither he nor any of his friends wanted to go on camera again. They had told their experiences once, they said, and had no desire for further publicity. This is consistent with the behavior of most other witnesses, I might add.

The Witness Conundrum

The Reed City sightings are a perfect illustration of the ecstasy and the agony of eyewitness sightings. Without people who are willing to take the time to contact a researcher and risk public ridicule, there would be no sightings reported, and most investigations into the nature of cryptid animals would cease. I believe the great majority of creature sighting reports come from credible, ordinary people who have seen something extraordinary in the course of their daily travels and activities. They seldom want anything more than additional information or perhaps validation. Some even say they feel they have a duty to report their experience in order to help the research.

There is a very small percentage of "witnesses," however, who either invent a tale completely or become obsessed with a questionable photo or video and then seek publicity for their bogus claims.

Hoaxers' motives can range from a desire to have some fun at the expense of others to a malicious intent to make a researcher look foolish. Some even hope to profit by inventing a cryptid character to serve as a base for sales of CDs, T-shirts, bobbleheads, you name it. Want to spike sales of your Jersey Devil T-shirt? Spawn a few new sightings, get Channel 92 to put it on the evening news! Auction your blobby photo on eBay! Make a faked video!

Unfortunately, it's the latter group that gets most of the mainstream press—and who are most often invoked by skeptics as the reason to disbelieve the other 97 percent of reports. The problem lies in weeding them out. A few are easy to discern, but in the end, the evaluation of any creature incident depends entirely upon the honesty of its eyewitnesses.

In the "American Werewolf" episode of *MonsterQuest,* the producers addressed the uncertainty of witness testimony by asking the witnesses to take polygraph tests administered by a specialist from the Minnesota area. They were limited to those witnesses who were within close traveling range of Delavan, Wisconsin, where the expert was set up at a motel. Not one of the witnesses tested declined or even hesitated to be tested, and all seven people received results of "no deception detected." The producers couldn't even fit them all into the final cut of the show.

Of course, that only proves that they believe they saw what they reported, but what all of these people reported was something very hard to explain. And so are many of the sightings that have come my way since then. Since it is impossible for me to administer polygraph tests to all those who contact me, I simply do my best to report what the witness said and what I know about the person, the place, and anything else that seems important. Readers can then make their own decisions about the veracity of each witness and the possible nature of what each one claimed to see.

Whatever that is, one thing is clear. "If (as Ray Parker Jr. says in his *Ghostbusters* theme song) there's something strange in your neighborhood...if there's something weird and it don't look good," people are gonna call. The rest of this book is devoted to them.

Chapter 2

Manwolves of the Manistee Region

John Lyons and his friends were not the only ones to report an upright, wolf-like creature in the Reed City area. A report that echoed their claim arrived in December, 2007, from a resident unrelated to the Lyons group. His sighting occurred about two miles north of the school-house sightings, near a chain of small lakes. Between the two sightings areas lies mostly undeveloped, sparsely populated rural land.

The year was about 1994, and the witness was a young teen at the time. He had a nightly habit of sneaking out of their rented farmhouse to smoke cigarettes behind the garage, facing a big, rotting barn. His habit was strong enough to draw him outdoors even on a snow-filled January night, the buildings ringed with high drifts.

He was turned toward the barn, he said, when he saw a dark shape poking out of a broken board in the barn wall. At first he thought it must be some unknown hunk of farm equipment, but as he continued to watch, the "equipment" moved. "It had a strange look to it," he wrote, "almost like it had eyes and large pointy ears, but I figured it was my imagination running wild. After all, this barn was quite a ways from where I was standing, and it was dark out so I just kept staring at it and smoking."

A noise coming from the nearby woods startled him, however, and he saw the "thing" turn its head to look, as well. "Last I checked," he said, "farm equipment does not move. After it turned its head to the noise, it turned right back to me. It had been watching me the whole time. I wasn't gonna take my eyes off it."

He estimated the creature stood six feet tall on its hind legs, and was dark in color. "It had a dog-like appearance," he said, "a pointy nose and really big pointy ears. It looked as if it kinda had a hunched back but like I said it was far away and it was dark and it was in a barn. I walked backwards into the house because I was terrified to turn my back to the thing even though it was too far away to catch me that fast."

Once inside, he said, he grabbed a flashlight and, hands trembling, told his mother what he had seen. Predictably, she did not believe him. He ran back outside and trained the flashlight on the barn from a safe distance, but the creature was no longer there. He checked for footprints in the snow the next day but there were none, leading him to wonder if it might still be in the barn. He also noticed that the drift where the creature had stood was more than three feet high, and the creature stood four to five feet higher than that.

The witness said he considered—and discarded—the possible explanations: it was the wrong shape for a bear, too big and bipedal to be a dog, and too cold for some neighbor to be playing tricks on him.

A female friend also saw something strange outside that house while visiting after that incident. "She just started crying one night," he said, "and it took me hours to get her to tell me...she just said, 'I seen something the size of a buffalo and it looked like a dog and I don't want to talk about it anymore.' I knew what she had seen. I didn't tell her I had seen it too, she was already too scared as it was."

He said that while he did not see the creature again, his family was concerned that pets, especially cats, began to go missing. At the time, he said he had never heard of the Dogman legend and didn't know that other people near Reed City had seen the creature until he saw my account of it online.

(Again, I am keeping the identities of witnesses private if I have the slightest doubt that they want to go public or if their name has not already been identified elsewhere.)

Hunting Horror

Another unrelated report of a Reed City area sighting came from a deer hunter who was nearly scared out of his tree stand in November, 2007. Sam (I'm using just his first name at his request) was twenty at the time, and hunting with two companions who were stationed at separate spots. The time was 4:30 p.m., with dusk approaching. Sam was getting ready to head in when he noticed the birds suddenly became quiet and he could see nothing moving at all.

The stillness was broken when two does and a buck moved uneasily through the clearing Sam was watching. After noticing a foul smell that reminded him of old mothballs, he was shocked to see an entirely different animal enter the clearing. It was large, dark-furred, and walked on two feet, "not like a bear but more like a hunch-back," he said. "A bear can't walk that fast on two feet, not to mention run," he added.

The creature continued running on two feet through the clearing, presumably after the deer, and then finally dropped to all fours to continue its pursuit through the woods. It had upright, pointed ears, Sam said, and the body was sleeker than that of a wolf, although broader in some areas. It stood about six feet tall on two legs and had a muzzle similar to that of a Husky dog.

Sam decided to stay put until his friends came to pick him up in their truck. They laughed at his story until Sam pointed out the tracks the animal left in the snow. The tracks resembled those of a dog "but broader," he said. "Four toes were visible with about two-inch claws leading them (made separate impressions in the dirt and mud)." The front paw prints where the creature dropped onto all fours measured five inches long by two-three inches wide, and the rear paws measured seven inches long by three-and-one-half inches wide.

Could it have been a bear? The track measurements come close to the size a very large black bear could leave, but a bear track shows five toes. Sam is also correct in guessing that a bear would not have run through the clearing on two feet. Bears will rear upright when surprised or when looking at something, but they do not travel bipedally as a rule. Even if they did, their loping gait and big hindquarters make them fairly easy to recognize, especially at close range by an experienced outdoorsman. It would also seem unreasonable to describe a bear as "sleeker than a wolf."

But that is not the end of the story.

On the second day of the hunt, Sam could not make himself go out in the dark morning hours and stayed behind until about two in the afternoon, when he decided to arm himself more heavily and try again. He took a pistol, knife, and a semi-automatic rifle and went to sit in his tree. The afternoon was uneventful until around dark at five p.m. when he heard three shots about 100 yards away and sounds of screaming came from his walkie-talkie earpiece. He climbed down to find one of his companions running at him after having seen the same creature Sam saw the day before. Sam's friend also described it as dark-furred, with yellow eyes, and said that it left the same footprints.

The pair stayed in for the third day of their hunt while their third friend hunted and saw nothing out of the ordinary. Thinking that perhaps the animal had left the area, they all hunted on the fourth day, but Sam and the other witness shared Sam's blind this time, neither wishing to be alone.

They were not alone.

No sooner had they settled in than the creature ran upright into the clearing in the dim morning light, this time aware of their presence and staring directly at them, "almost grinning," said Sam.

They noted that its arms seemed as long as a human's. Sam's buddy pulled his weapon and the creature immediately changed course and ran into the woods, making a "growl/hissing noise." The pair sat tight, waiting to see if it would come back.

About an hour later, their other friend called on the walkie-talkie from his blind and asked, "Um, you guys, are you in a werewolf suit at my blind? Because it's not funny." Five shots immediately followed.

Sam and his friend scrambled down the tree, hopped in their truck, and raced to pick up their now-believing companion. He was shaking as he showed them his gun stock which had claw marks on it!

The creature had charged him, he said, and he shot the first round almost accidentally as he tried to block the attack. The noise scared it back into the woods, and he fired the other rounds hoping to keep it away.

The three rode back to their cabin where they found more of the same tracks and claw marks by the door. They decided to grab their belongings, abandon their blinds and leave, although they had planned to stay seven days. As they left, they felt something slam into the rear of their truck, but it was dark by then and they never saw what it was.

Sam said he later tried to tell a DNR agent about the creature, but said, "He just thought I was nuts so I never made an official report. I'm actually thinking about abandoning my blind; I'm scared to death to go back there."

Suffice it to say that the additional sightings lend much more credence to the Lyons incident, especially since the hunting encounter occurred within a year of the sightings at the old schoolhouse. The fact that the other Reed City event, the farm sighting, occurred in 1994 suggests the creature has some history here. And as would be expected in that case, Dogman reports flow in from the wildlife-rich surrounding area, too.

Manistee Mysteries

Only about five miles northwest of Reed City lurk the thousands of acres of woods of the Pere Marquette State Forest which, together with the adjacent Huron-Manistee National Forest, comprises almost a *mil-*

lion acres of wild land. That is one whopping chunk of wildlife cover. It is difficult to believe that the dense growth of evergreen, oak, and many other types of trees was once clear-cut by the lumber industry, then replanted after an attempt to lure farmers failed. Even though the wide-scale habitat destruction must have been devastating for the animals that lived there, today the forest teems with known species of wildlife: from deer and ruffed grouse to large predators such as bears. And if witnesses are to be believed, it has also regained a few unknown species. The land is a continuing source of strange creature sightings.

The word "Manistee" is from the Ojibwe for "spirit of the forest." That seems appropriate since for many years people have been seeing something here that acts unlike any known natural animal. In *The Beast of Bray Road,* I recounted the old logging camp tale of two lumbermen fishing near Manistee who were accosted in their boat by a swimming, dog-like creature, and the story of Robert Fortney who stared down a grinning, bipedal dog after shooting a member of its pack in self defense in Mecosta County in 1938, for starters.

The forest range stretches almost as far north as Traverse City and southward to Muskegon County, ranging several counties eastward as it goes. In *Hunting the American Werewolf,* I told the story of Tammy Moss, who saw an upright, furry dog-like creature cross the road and then realized yellow eyes were glaring at her from seven feet above the ground, just north of Traverse City in 1989 or '90.

It was just a year earlier, in 1988, that Daniel Wrzesinski, who is now a reporter for the *Manistee News Advocate,* had made it his summer mission to drive the highways and back roads of the forest until he found the Dogman made famous in Cook's "Legend" the previous decade. He and a friend, Tony, thought nothing of jouncing along rugged two-track lanes in very secluded areas in the wee hours of the morning, bolstering their nerves with *Dead Can Dance* blasting from the car's speakers. They were further intrigued as local papers had reported cattle found killed by some large predator.

The road on which the pair received their fright, however, was no muddy forest trail but Highway M55: a well-trafficked straight shot through the Manistee National Forest. They were following a line of several other cars, Wrzesinski wrote me in 2006, when they spotted "a creature that moved partially upright" crossing the road ahead of them. Silhouetted in the headlights of at least three cars, it appeared to be a "skinny, furry creature." It moved more like a human would than an animal, he said, "not unlike a baboon," with long limbs. Its shape was totally unlike a bear, he said, and it was much too big to be a coyote or ordinary dog.

The creature melted into the blackness of the ditch alongside the road as Wrzesinski slammed on his brakes, and by the time he could manage a u-turn for a second look, it was gone. The pair were so unnerved they decided to just go back home. He was sure the occupants of the other vehicles also had to have seen it and often wonders what they thought about the odd creature.

I also received a second-hand report of another sighting, told to me by researcher Mark Curtiss, which occurred just north of Ludington, Mason County, in April, 1997. A female friend of his, Lola, and her uncle, Jim, were hiking on the Lake Michigan shore near the Manistee National Forest campground at about 11 p.m., under a full moon. As they picked their way along the shoreline, they saw what looked like a large log lying on the water's edge about fifty feet ahead of them. As they walked toward it, they were shocked to see the "log" jump up and stand on two feet, staring back at them as they felt the hackles rise on their necks.

The creature was the first to take action. It sprang to the side and began running away from them at great speed, heading north along the shoreline and then eastward over the dunes. The whole incident was over in seconds, leaving both Lola and Jim shaken as they realized how vulnerable they had been, coming so close to the large beast.

Lola and Jim have slightly different memories of the event; Jim recalls the creature dropping to all fours as it ran away over the dunes while Lola thought it stayed in a bipedal mode. They both estimated it as four to five feet tall (shorter than most manwolf or dogman reports) and covered with short, dark fur. They did find footprints and described them as dog-like, with claws, but with a "strange shape" replacing the usual toe pads. (Dog-like prints with claw points would rule out a small Bigfoot.)

When they returned to camp and told relatives about their encounter, their family informed them they had just seen the Michigan Dogman. Neither had ever heard of it at that point. Curtiss added that both Lola and Jim were "hard-working, successful people" with no prior interest in strange creatures. He made his own research trip to the campground, and while he did not encounter any dogmen, he did learn from a local news photographer that a trapper had recently found very large wolf tracks just south of Ludington. (It is not at all unlikely that a gray wolf could wander into that area.)

Golf Cart at the Crossroads

Closer to Dogman Central near Baldwin and Little Star Lake in July, 2004, two twelve-year-olds were out for a summer joyride on a golf cart on a private rural road. Acting with good safety consciousness, the pair stopped at a crossroads and looked both ways before proceeding. Although they did not see any approaching vehicles, they did spot the silhouette of what looked like a large dog running along the road on four legs.

As they squinted at it, to their amazement the creature rose up onto its hind legs and continued on that way. As the writer said in her email of August 22, 2006, "We had never seen anything like it! It was so skinny and tall to be a bear and it obviously wasn't a man because it had been running on four legs very fast, nothing like the speed of a man. My friend doesn't like to talk about it and she tries to forget about it."

The writer added that she cannot listen to Cook's "The Legend" "because the thoughts of a dogman running around in the woods just downright scares me."

Uninvited Vacationer

A more bizarre Manistee incident came from a Kentucky man who happened to be vacationing at a secluded cabin near Manistee in 2003 or 2004 with his wife and her parents when they all glimpsed something unexpected.

The man and his wife arrived around dusk to find his in-laws already there. His wife immediately ran into the cabin but he took a few minutes to stretch and look around. He noticed a wide path into the woods—and something walking on the path only 30-40 yards away! It walked on all fours and seemed dog-like but larger than any dog or wolf. It moved in absolute silence but paused when it saw the man and stared at him, grimacing as if making a soundless hiss.

The man was so fatigued from the twelve-hour drive he had just made that he turned away and ignored the creature to begin unloading their vehicle! A few minutes later, his in-laws surprised him by popping out of the woods on that same path where he had just seen the large quadruped. They had also encountered it, coming back from the opposite direction after hiking with their dog. They watched as it ran away into a field and affirmed that it was huge, dog-like, but moved smoothly like a big cat.

Of course, it did not walk upright but one feature of dogmen or manwolves noted by many witnesses is that they are able to switch between two-footed and four-footed modes very easily. Although I don't always publish strictly four-footed sightings, I will include some in this book, particularly when the sighting occurs near other reported incidents.

In this case, the animal was so large and unusual, the man wondered if it might be a left-over dire wolf, an animal with massive teeth and a bit more size than the average gray wolf. It was well-distributed across the North American continent during the last Ice Age, and has been extinct for several thousand years. Could some have survived over the millennia in the Manistee National Forest? Unless one is captured, we may never know.

I also must note that there are no indications from fossil skeletons of *Canis dirus* that it walked upright, so it still would not necessarily explain the other Manistee sightings. And there is one other report that is unexplainable by any standards.

The Ravenna Scrabbler

On January 3, 2004, four young men aged 12-17 decided to take a winter's night walk through the woods belonging to one of their parents just outside of Ravenna in Muskegon County. They were only a few miles southeast of the Muskegon State Game Area, which lies nearly adjacent to the southernmost tip of the Manistee National Forest.

They followed a trail through the still and silent woods to where the property line ended, and there they all began to smell an overpowering stench that the writer said, "I can only associate with death which is odd because (the air) was roughly 30 degrees Fahrenheit, a temperature at which even rotting flesh should be frozen and absent of smell."

Next, they began to hear something moving through the brush as if it were circling them. "This put us on edge," he wrote, "and my brother and his friend, the younger two in the group, were losing composure. I decided to loop around and exit down a trail parallel to the one we entered on. I knew this trail very well and was confident on it due to the lack of tree top coverage which allowed the moonlight to illuminate it just enough for me to have the upper hand in the event we were being stalked."

The four stuck together on the new trail, with only one flashlight between them. They had made it about half way back when they all stopped in their tracks. Scrabbling at the snow and leaves at the base of a deer blind about fifteen feet away from them was a whitish-colored humanoid creature that stood up to face them on two legs. It was about three to four feet tall, naked and furless with humanlike hands. Its head was round and humanlike, but the light was not bright enough to show the facial features.

After both parties stared in shock for a few seconds, the creature dropped to all fours and took off down another trail at what looked like an incredible speed. The four young men turned and ran in the opposite direction as fast as they were able.

The witness said the creature reminded him most of the character Gollum in the film version of *The Lord of the Rings*.

"Upon discussing it we had all seen the same thing and could not understand what it was and what it was doing. I mean a creature with no fur, no clothing, and stringy like this thing could not possibly be that active in below (freezing) temperatures."

At my request, the man's younger brother sent me his own written statement of the events. His account tallied very well with the account above, with one addition. He remembered the creature emitting a "scream-like," high-pitched sound as it ran away. He also added that it was close enough as it scrambled for cover that he could be sure it was not a human playing a prank. He also affirmed that the four of them ran for their house in a terrified all-out sprint.

Five years later, the brothers hope to spend some time searching to see whether the creature still lives in his parents' woods. Given the extreme strangeness of the situation, I am not sure if I should wish them luck in finding it.

The only natural explanation I can think of might be a coyote with mange—it would stand about the right height—but it would not have had hands or a round, humanoid head. It would also seem odd that a coyote would have exuded such a noticeable stench.

The Manistee National Forest area does teem with creature strangeness, and it shares a common feature I'd noticed with Midwestern sightings in general. Encounters not only usually happen near a water source, but tend to aggregate in areas adjacent to the Great Lakes. It is almost as if these waterways form the basis of a migratory route that circles east to New York and then follows the Mississippi River south and also forks to a lesser degree to the west into Iowa and Oklahoma.

But there are ample sightings of upright, dog-like creatures in the rest of Michigan, including the eastern side of the state along Lake Huron and the more populated areas south of Muskegon. I had one brief report from Conklin in Ottawa County in August, 2009, that described a large, dog-like creature spotted walking on its hind legs by two boys as they were shining for raccoons just north of town near a creek and bike trail. The dogman likes to range through his entire home state, it seems, and remains busy claiming new territory.

Chapter 3

Michigan's Eastern Enigmas

One of my favorite stories in *Hunting the American Werewolf*—just for its sheer, innards-emptying sense of terror—was that of the "Repo Man." Jeff Cornelius encountered a very menacing upright dogman in the summer of 2005 on lonely Fish Lake Road south of Holly as he went about his business of attempting to repossess someone's truck.

As he peered into a shed, he heard a noise behind him and swiveled to see a huge, upright dogman coming straight for him. He barely made it back into his own vehicle in time. This was no bored teenager looking for thrills; Cornelius was a grown man who had never heard of the dogman until he was informed by his coworkers after telling them what he saw.

Deer Chase, Interrupted

Interestingly, someone else saw something similar in that same northern tier of Oakland County, just a few townships away near the tiny berg of Oxford. It happened in the summer of 1996—nine years before Cornelius' encounter—to a woman who wishes to remain anonymous. "Zoe" said she was driving home late one night on Ray Road, with the radio blaring her favorite tunes, when she had to slam on the brakes to avoid hitting two deer hell-bent on crossing the road in front of her.

She skidded to a stop on the dirt road, then was shocked to see that the deer were followed by a "wolf-or-dog-like creature." The animal was making loud snarling and growling noises, but it stopped at the front passenger corner of her vehicle and stared.

"The wolf creature sat there for about fifteen-twenty seconds studying and growling at me," she said, "when I noticed it was not a normal dog or wolf, as it had a human body! It was standing on two legs, hunched over, and its head was higher than the roof of my car."

The creature was covered in dark brown, matted fur an inch or two long. She also noticed the ears very distinctly because they reminded her of her own dogs—Bouvier des Flandres—with "prick style ears with tufts of hair on the edges."

Its eyes, reflecting the light of the headlights (which rules out a human in a suit), were brownish yellow.

Zoe said that it took a few moments for her brain to process that information, and then she stepped on the gas. To her horror, it lunged after her car. After a few seconds, however, she saw in her rear-view mirror that it had resumed its pursuit of the deer and was running off into the field—on two legs.

Zoe kept her story mostly to herself but decided to write me after seeing the "American Werewolf" episode of *MonsterQuest*. "To this day when I go by or down that road," she wrote me in January, 2008, "I still remember what happened and what I saw that night."

On a strange, final note, it was only a few years ago that she happened to watch an episode of the British science fiction show, *Doctor Who*, titled "Tooth and Claw." It was about a werewolf, and the show's computer-generated monster was shockingly close to what she saw on Ray Road.

"I'm so glad to know I'm not the only one who had that type of encounter in that area," she said. "That means I am not crazy!"

The instructive thing about the Holly sightings is that although the region is rich in lakes, rivers, farm fields and recreation areas, it is only a county removed from Detroit, whose northern suburbs actually do spread into Oakland County.

The Rochester Hill Monster

Another very close Oakland County encounter came from Rochester, which lies only a few miles east of Pontiac. Jerry Falkner, an auto worker employed by Chrysler for twenty-four years, saw the creature in the summer of 1982 when he was still in high school. His sighting occurred on Sheldon Road, which runs north out of Rochester between the Ball Mountain Recreation Area and the Stony Creek Metropolitan Park. He wrote to me in March, 2009, and I interviewed him at length.

"It was early spring, about 50 degrees out," he told me, "and at the time there was an old gravel pit we called 'The Hill.' There were holes and construction dig-outs, and the Paint Creek ran through there into the Clinton River. Oakland County was more blue-collar then.

"I was hanging out with my buddies around 10:30-11:00 p.m. with a bonfire—we were four-wheeling, not drinking or smoking—and I had walked to the other side of a pile of shingles to go to the bathroom. I knew there was something standing behind me; I just turned around and had a big shock. It was a foot from my face."

Jerry found himself staring into the yellowish eyes of an upright, dog-like creature. Its "arms" were at its side, and he had the feeling it was "checking him out."

"If those arms would have come up, I'd have fainted," he added.

He estimated it stood over seven feet tall, since the six-foot Jerry stood elevated on the pile of debris and he was face-to-face with the creature as its tongue lolled over one side of its jaw. Its waist was tapered and it appeared to have thick shoulders.

"It had a huge head, shaggy dark brown fur from the shoulders down—so thick it looked almost like a cape. It looked more like a dog. I could see its teeth. The teeth were canine. I could feel and smell its breath. It smelled musky or gamy."

Jerry's friends had been preparing to leave and were already waiting for him in his Jeep about forty feet away. Jerry made a mad dash for the car.

"I ran as fast as I could," he said, "it was horrible. I didn't look back."

That was just as well, since the creature was chasing him on two feet. Jerry made it into the car and took off, and the creature followed them for about a quarter of a mile, alternating between two and four feet, before disappearing into the brush.

Jerry still wonders what, exactly, it was.

"No way it was a wolf standing up," he said. "I've hunted my whole life and have seen wolves. Till this day I have never been that terrified. Never in my life did I think things like that existed. I have the chills right now, twenty-seven years later."

The gravel pit is no longer there, said Jerry. A high school was built in the area, which has been generally improved since then. But he and his buddies never went four-wheeling there again.

Nor are other southeastern areas of Michigan exempt from weird canine behavior.

At Wit's End in DeWitt

Clinton County sits in the center of the southern half of the lower peninsula, barely north of the major transportation hub that is Lansing. The community of DeWitt is only a few miles north of the county border, but it also lies just south of the Muskrat Lake State Game Area. Numerous rivers and other small lakes make the mostly rural area a fisherman's haven.

One DeWitt woman wrote to me that in the summer of 2008, she and her husband fished almost daily until around two in the afternoon, when he had to get ready to go to his second-shift job. Their favorite spot was at Babcock's Landing on the Looking Glass River, which cuts a wiggly east-west swath across the bottom of the county and passes through the center of DeWitt. Babcock's Landing in Victor Township is known for its pike fishing and is an "unimproved" launch used only for canoes and car-top boats. It is very close to the little Round Lake and lies between Sleepy Hollow State Park to the north and the Rose Lake Wildlife Research Area to the south.

Again, a combination of water and game areas makes this prime critter country.

The couple fished from shore that warm and sunny day and left at their usual time. They were making the short drive north to Round Lake Road when something large, furry and black crossed Babcock Road about one hundred yards ahead.

"It came from the driver's side to the right side of the road," she said. "It was completely black in the sunlight. My husband slowed down to almost a crawl, but as we went past we could not see where it went in the swampy grass. The rest of the way home we tried to figure out what it was we had just seen."

Her husband tried to convince himself it was just a dog, she said, "but I knew it wasn't; it was too big and not built right."

The creature was not upright, and its profile reminded her of a hyena. "Its front legs and shoulders seemed bigger and stood higher than the back legs. The neck and chest area seemed to be covered with thicker, longer hair almost like a mane. (This sounds very much like the Hill Monster encountered by Jerry in Rochester.) Unable to decide what it was, they finally put it out of their minds—until it happened again.

It was a year later, on the last weekend of July, 2009, when they again set off for a day of fishing at Babcock's Landing. They noticed as they drove the back roads that many of the roadside swamps were swollen from the wetter-than-usual summer. The woman had just resigned herself to the fact that the river was probably too high for fishing, when she saw "another one of those things" jump into the road ahead of them, only about twenty feet away this time.

"Going from the left to the right it disappeared into the tall grass on the passenger side of the road," she said. "It was so fast it was barely a glimpse, and I couldn't believe it could leap the road in one bound." The woman craned to look for it in the grass, but it disappeared almost instantly, melting into the landscape.

The only thing different about this second sighting, she noted, was that the black fur was marbled with brown and reddish brown.

"I was wondering now if there is a whole population of these things running around here," she wondered (justifiably, I think). "This was not a black bear, a coyote, or anything else we are familiar with! I seriously don't want to run into one while I'm deer hunting!"

The He-Man Dog

One sighting in that southeastern quadrant of the state contained an observation that most witnesses don't ever seem to notice; evidence of the creature's sex.

Cycle back a few decades to the summer of '73 (summer seems to be the main sightings season for this area), to the Flint area in Genesee County. I will call the witness "Jim." He was between his sophomore and junior year in high school, he wrote, and often passed the time riding around delivering fruit and other produce with his Uncle Jay, who drove for a company called Pampania's. He was staying with his aunt and uncle for the summer. At the end of each night's rounds the pair would return the company truck to a fenced lot, and Jay would drive them home in his own car.

It was about 11:30 p.m. one Thursday night as they drove up the hilly, winding drive to the truck park that Jay and Jim both caught sight of a large, dog-like animal pawing at something on the side of the road. It paid no notice to the approaching truck, and as they came closer to it, Jim could see the creature rooting and licking at something with its tongue and snout.

Then, he wrote, "The S.O.B. stood up!"

Jim's uncle slowed the truck and flashed the high beams at the creature, giving Jim the shock of his life. What he saw was a man's powerful, upright body which was covered in black fur and topped off with the head of a wolf-like canine. The creature peered at them with eyes that reflected yellow in the headlights. Jim also noticed an unmistakably prominent male organ.

Jay kept the truck moving slowly past the strange beast, which then leaped across the road in one long bound.

After trading off vehicles, Jay and Jim started back down the hill, eyes wide open. To Jim's horror, his uncle stopped the car where the creature had stood, grabbed a handgun from under his seat, and got out to have a look. What he found there was evidently the creature's dinner—a half-eaten deer carcass. Jim said they watched for the dogman all the rest of that summer but were never favored with another glimpse.

Ann Arbor Window Peeper

Some encounters are more eerie than dramatic. In nearby Ann Arbor, Washtenaw County, a young man reported seeing something like a German shepherd or wolf that stood six feet tall staring into the window of a pole barn on the property of a house that he was visiting, around 2004. He said the creature was leaning over slightly to peer into a six-paned, chest-high window. The property where this occurred backed up to a marshy wooded area directly behind the barn. The writer said his family often had strange feelings that the creature was around.

And while I'm not chronicling Bigfoot reports in this book, I feel I should mention that a controversial flap of sightings of a creature known as the Monroe Monster occurred just south of Detroit, near the Lake Erie city of Monroe. Reports of the creature, generally described as similar to what we now call Bigfoot, began as early as the 1930s and continued to the mid-60s when two women claimed to be attacked in their car by a seven-foot-tall hairy monster.

Even Detroit has a long history of *loup-garou* tales dating back to the city's first French inhabitants in the 1700s.

Altogether, there's a surprisingly solid and ever-accumulating pile of reports from Michigan's southeastern corner. But perhaps they have only followed a trail from the state's southwestern parts...

Chapter 4

Kalamazoo and Dogman Too

In *Hunting the American Werewolf*, I noted my discovery that many hot spots of Wisconsin manwolf sightings dovetailed with the locations of certain animal-shaped effigy mounds left by ancient, indigenous people. It's very tempting to imagine that the makers of these mounds left some type of spirit guardians (in the shape of dogmen, perhaps?) to watch over their sacred spots.

I found it fascinating, then, to discover that southwestern Michigan has its own ancient, unexplained earth formations—in the same general areas where many creature sightings have occurred. Called "garden beds" because their geometric shapes reminded Yankee settlers of formal English gardens, we know about them only from surveys and drawings made before farmers plowed them under. But they were as magnificent as they were mysterious.

Found chiefly in Cass, St. Joseph and Kalamazoo Counties, mostly along the Grand and St. Joseph River valleys, the "garden beds" covered hundreds of acres, according to historian Bela Hubbard in an 1878 article in *American Antiquarian*. Some were as big as 100 feet across. They were laid out in precisely divided circles, rectangle and arrowhead shapes, and were already abandoned hundreds of years before European settlers arrived. The Potawatomi people living there said that the mounds were made by "Prairie People" they called *Yam-Ko-Desh*—and warned that their "spirits" still guarded their ancient sites.

Ancient formations and spirits aside, Michigan's southwestern portion is a well-populated area known for its fruit crops. It is as lavishly watered as the rest of the state, and perhaps that is why it is also prone to reports of strange canines.

Creature of the Corn

Sturgis is the largest city in St. Joseph County, and so far south is almost touches the Indiana border. It lies surrounded by a constellation of small lakes, and it was near one of these that a young woman and several male friends had a strange interaction with something that came panting out of a cornfield in late summer, around 1986.

At about 2:00 a.m., the group was walking home from a casual party along a road the woman has asked me not to identify, when they first heard some sort of large animal exhaling in great huffs. They began to grow nervous as they realized it had exited the cornfield next to them and was crossing the road behind them. It continued to keep pace from the other side, hidden by woods and shrubs.

Viewing conditions were less than ideal; it was a warm, humid night with scant moonlight. Straining to see in the dark, they caught only glimpses of whatever stalked them. One of those glimpses was of an upright, man-sized figure standing next to a tree as they passed. Another time they spotted a pair of yellowish eyes watching them. One of the young men finally picked up a rock and hurled it into the field in the direction of the panting noise. They heard a soft thud and then a yelp like an injured dog would make. Then the animal began to growl—loudly.

The woman and her friends ran, making it safely to the house; they still talk about that incident between themselves twenty years later. The woman admitted they had each had a few drinks, but were not drunk, and all of them perceived the same things.

A witness's state of sobriety is something I like to establish in any report, and of course any hint of inebriation raises the pooh-pooh factor in the minds of skeptics. But the walkers in this story don't sound terribly impaired—they were able to observe, throw a rock accurately and run—and the fact that they all shared the same experience rules out individual hallucinations.

I've also seen statements questioning why a certain number of witnesses seem to be "bored young people," with the inference that they are inventing their tales for fun. That could certainly be true in some cases, but the fact is that people who party late at night in isolated places have simply put themselves in a more likely spot for observing any kind of creatures of the night.

Other people who have reason to drive late at night—third shift workers, travelers, emergency and health care workers, to name a few—make up another large chunk of witnesses. Simon Thalmann of the *Kalamazoo Gazette*, who wrote an article about my appearance at the Kalamazoo Public Library, passed on a letter he received from a woman shortly after I was there.

Portage Possum-Player

Early in September, 2008, she wrote, at about 10:00 p.m., she was tooling along Highland Drive en route to her home on Austin Lake. The night was both rainy and foggy, so she was keeping a close eye on the road. Near Zylman Road, she caught sight of something large lying on the pavement ahead of her. As she slowed to avoid running it over, she was astonished to see the fur-covered body jump up and begin to run away on two feet.

"It turned its head toward me and I saw this furry, weird face," she wrote. Her first thought was whether it could be a person dressed up as an animal—but then wondered why any trickster would choose such a desolate place and such terrible weather, not to mention the dangerous act of lying down in the middle of a wet road.

She called the Portage Police when she arrived at her house, which was less than a mile from the incident. She never heard back from the police, and her family laughed at her story. However, the sight of the creature really scared her, she said, and she now refuses to walk alone at night in her neighborhood.

The Creepy Crawler

People who do drive regularly at night are usually on automatic lookout for deer. A man driving home to Hickory Corners between Kalamazoo and Battle Creek at about 2:50 a.m. the night of July 1, 2006, thought that the animal at the edge of the road ahead of him was just that—a deer—until he realized it was standing on two legs, staring at him with small round eyes.

He described it as a six-to-seven-foot-tall "man-animal," but too slender to be a man. He continued to approach the creature, and as he came closer, it suddenly dropped to all fours while the man passed it slowly.

"It looked like a large man lying dead on the side of the road, except it had fur and abnormally lanky, sloth-like arms."

The creature then used those long arms to drag itself commando-style into the adjacent cornfield.

"This creature went from standing six to seven feet tall," he said, "to low enough to hide in the short cornfield."

The corn did not stand even two feet high, he said, but when he spun his car around and came back for another look, he couldn't catch even a glimpse of it. He found my website later, he said, and was astonished that it matched exactly the descriptions of other witnesses and my drawing that I call "the indigenous dogman," which is a compilation sketch of the traits most witnesses claim to see. My drawing is of a very obviously canine creature, so I think that rules out the possibility it might have been a smaller Bigfoot.

His mother and two brothers had seen a creature of the same description earlier in the same area, and the family believes that they all saw the same thing.

Geographically, Hickory Corners lies northeast of Kalamazoo in Barry County and is surrounded by small lakes, only a few miles from Gull Lake. Plenty of water, cornfields and animals both wild and tame—plus the possibility of roadkill from two major north-south highways that pass to either side of the town—make this prime dogman territory.

Beast of Battle Creek

In the year 2000, twenty-eight-year-old Nelly (her nickname, used at the witness' request) worked in the Fort Custer Recreation Area, a 3,000-plus acreage six miles west of Battle Creek and only five or six miles south of Hickory Corners. Pregnant at the time, she was driving from Urbandale on Battle Creek's north side to her third shift job in late summer or early autumn. She rolled her car windows up tight and turned on the radio to keep herself company.

As Nelly wound along a dark road that led to a bridge over a branch of the Kalamazoo River about 10:30 p.m., she came to an intersection (Dickman and Clark) where she knew that if she made a turn to the right, she would come upon an old post cemetery. Instead, she looked straight ahead and saw what looked like a dog crossing the road on all fours. She slowed down for the animal but was not concerned—until it stood up and turned toward her as it reached the weeds on the shoulder. She stopped the car in front of the gray beast she estimated to be about the size of a black lab, and observed that it looked "miffed, mangy and mixed up," as it stood on its hind legs looking at her.

"The shape of its body was like a young boy," she told me in a phone interview on February 23, 2008, "and it was a little bigger than me and I'm five-foot-two. It had fur everywhere. As it stood up straight at full posture and looked at me, I got scared and drove off. An animal doesn't have emotions, but this animal seemed like it had emotions. It had weird eyes."

Trying to get a mental fix on the creature in her headlights only fifteen feet away, Nelly said she first wondered if it could be a kangaroo, but then she noticed it had a bushy tail more like that of a wolf.

"Its ears looked pointy and big as a (German) shepherd's, bigger than a Doberman's. The legs looked like a dog's. When it looked straight at me its nose looked shorter—pressed up—and it was not as hairy under the eyes. It seemed sad like it didn't know what I was. Its face looked more like a human's…I thought the poor thing was hungry."

She later added that it had something of a chin.

It seemed to use its arms as a human would, she said, and she had the impression it was foraging for food. Another car came, and Nelly drove away and left the creature behind—but with the eerie and sudden thought that it could jump on the roof of her car if it wanted to. Nelly drew several sketches of the animal, adding that if her art skills were better, she would have made it skinnier and with longer legs and a more "boyish" face.

She was not the first person in her family that claimed to encounter a strange creature. She said years before her sighting, her mother and brother were chased by a large "lizard" that pursued them on its hind legs, and later peered at them through the windows of their trailer home. It is possible that hearing of this experience might have predisposed

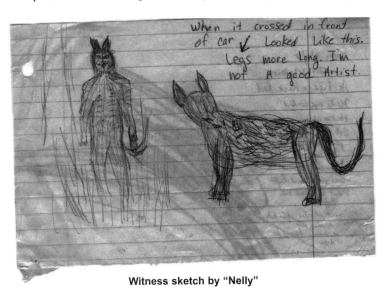

Witness sketch by "Nelly"

Nelly to look for something similar—or it may just have left her open to something that other drivers might have ignored or dismissed.

Nelly also wrote me a long letter detailing research she had done on mythic creatures as she continued to search for possible explanations of the enigma. I would like to note that many other witnesses have also told me that their experience is something they constantly think about and seek to understand.

The location of Nelly's sighting is interesting for a reason other than its nearness to ancient effigy sites. Fort Custer, now a busy industrial park, served as a heavily used military training base from 1917 to 1964 and still hosts the Army National Guard and a veteran's hospital. I have noted sightings of unknown, upright canines at other present or former military installations such as the Anubis-like creature seen at the Great Lakes Naval Base north of Chicago (*Hunting the American Werewolf*), or a wolf-like animal encountered by a snowmobiler near the old Fort Snelling in Minnesota.

Many people have asked me whether the manwolves might be some sort of super-soldier hybrids engineered by a secret government program. Do I even have to say this idea is not likely? It is true that medical science has made astonishing advances in creating human/animal chimeras, creatures that combine two distinct sets of DNA, in the lab, but I think it is safe to say science is far from the ability to produce an army of dogmen. Besides, who needs a soldier that has to be housebroken?

However, military fort locations are often chosen for the same qualities many ancient people looked for in their sacred sites: high ground and a great water supply. That means forts and holy grounds have probably often occupied the same places. And if there are such things as spirit guardians, conjured to protect old sites, perhaps they stay on even after the location's use has changed and pop out in their doggish forms from time to time to be seen by people like Nelly.

I realize some may find this explanation as outré as the idea of literal dog soldiers, but at least in the world of the supernatural—for those who accept it—there are no biological barriers such as inter-species incompatibility to prevent such a thing.

The Portage Panda

I could easily describe some reports that come my way as "inconvenient" and send them to the recycle basket to corrode for all eternity in the netherworlds of cyberspace. Who knows where dead emails really go?

A few are obvious jokes or hoaxes, of course, but if I have the sense that a report is coming from a real person who is sincerely trying to understand an experience, I hit save instead of delete. After all, today's questionably bizarre detail may be tomorrow's final puzzle piece.

One such tale came from a resident of Portage, a city that directly borders the southern edge of Kalamazoo. She had found me via Internet search engines after she and her daughter saw something unusual in an area cemetery and decided they wanted to report it. She did not explain what the two of them were doing in the cemetery after dark, nor did she provide a date, but she inferred the event was recent. I received the email June 4, 2008. She did not name the cemetery but said it was next to the city library, so it was probably the historic 1894 Central Cemetery, which also lies near a park complex.

Whatever the circumstances that led her there that night, she and her daughter heard rustling from the bushes beyond the fence at the back of the cemetery. They went to have a look and saw a creature on the other side of the fence. It was very dark in color with a white patch on its chest and a "very stout flat head." What it most resembled, she said, was a panda bear!

The animal was rocking from side to side and grunting. The woman said she felt it would harm them if they came closer, and she and her daughter quickly left the cemetery.

"I do feel it is some sort of protector," she wrote, "but I hope I never encounter another one."

Although the woman felt there was a spiritual dimension to her encounter, the creature itself did nothing overtly supernatural. Yet I doubt that it was an actual panda. Pandas are rare creatures in the United States, even among zoos, and require very specific habitats and food to survive. All I can do is chalk this one up as another example of unexplained creature weirdness in the land of the ancient garden bed plains.

Chapter 5

Beasts of the Bay and the U.P.—Unexplained

Michigan's Saginaw Bay area on Lake Huron is a fishing haven close to the Shiawassee National Wildlife Refuge, with about 9,500 acres of varied terrain from forest to marsh, just south of Saginaw. A few area residents have learned that the bay's wildlife is wild, indeed.

At the northernmost limits of the bay, the city of Oscoda is known as the home of a very real but extremely tiny "monster"—the Frisbee-shaped, tentacled BAV1 bacteria. It has the ability to eat vinyl chloride, a type of toxic waste, which makes it a useful monster, indeed.

Gremlin of the Old Gunnery

It was to the west of Oscoda, in November, 1977, when a hunter encountered an entirely different type of monster in a former US Air Force training area known locally as "the old gunnery range." (Again, with the former military sites!) The densely forested area near M-65 and Old Bissonette Road had earned a reputation as a place where hunters often lost their way.

The hunter had settled himself under some jack pines to watch a deer path he'd found, when at around 2:00 p.m. he heard movements behind him. When he turned around to see if it was a deer, the rustling sound also moved, but in such a way that it uncannily stayed behind him, out of his line of vision. It continued for over half an hour.

"My first impressions," said the man, "were (that it was a) stupid cousin (one of his hunting companions), bear, mountain lion, or some dumb hunter walking in circles. I was getting spooked, so I got up and slowly walked back to the two-track road, and the 'noise' followed me. I called out, 'If this is a joke, it's not funny, and I am armed to the teeth and...I am a marksman.'"

The mysterious sounds continued, and the hunter decided to move on whatever it was. He cut to the right at a bend in the road, dropped his vest and hat, and hid next to a tree in a thicket. Finally he was able to spot movement to go with the noise as some brush rustled fifty yards away. With his 30.06 rifle at the ready, he prepared to fire.

"What happened next seemed like an eternity," he said, "but only 20-30 seconds really elapsed." What he saw stunned him.

"It was something out of the *Predator* movie," he said. "I could see a form, large, at least seven feet tall, but it was translucent. 'It' stopped and was facing my direction."

He tossed a rock toward it and it moved slightly. He shot five rounds at it and was sure that he hit it, and the creature moved as if in surprise. However, since the creature didn't seem very affected, the hunter pulled out a 357 magnum pistol and fired three six-round speed loaders.

"I was a police officer at this time and shot 600 on the combat course. No one on earth can tell me I missed." But the creature still had not fallen.

Dropping his rifle as dead weight, he began to run down the hill and soon met up with his hunting buddies who had heard all the shots and had come looking for him on their four-wheelers. Overcome by the fear of what he had seen, the hunter knelt and lost his lunch. But with vehicles and reinforcements, he agreed to go back and show them where he had seen the spooky thing. Something physical had been there; small trees and branches had been bent in a wide swath for 300 yards.

The group did report the event to the county sheriff's department, which dispatched the DNR to investigate. The DNR officer informed the man he must have seen a bear. But this hunter wasn't buying that explanation.

"It ain't no bear, or man, or Bigfoot," he wrote. "It's something else, indeed."

Another detail the man recalled after I questioned him further was that before the sighting, he had noticed that the woods were eerily silent, absent of the sounds of birds and squirrels. He also felt as if he was being watched before he saw the creature. When he saw it, he added, "It was like the forest opened up. The shape was tall, not wide. It really did not show arms or legs, it looked like a hole in the woods. It kind of absorbed all color and light, yet at the same time was not a shadow.

"It was like those badges that show two different things if you look at them from different angles; one angle was forest, the other was this hole.

"The only noise it made was when it walked, kind of soft rustling footfalls. Even when I shot it, it made no noise. It had no smell or odor."

It was not until years later, in 1987, that the *Predator* movie starring Arnold Schwarzenegger was released, and the hunter recalled his shock at seeing very nearly the same phenomenon before him on the screen.

Truthfully, this incident is far from a classic dogman sighting. A shimmering hole in the forest is not the same thing as a canine form. It sounds more like a typical description of a "portal" or opening from our world to something beyond, such as those told of by visitors to "Skinwalker Ranch" in *Hunt for the Skinwalker* by Colm A. Kelleher and George Knapp. But the thing was tall, with enough of a corporeal body to leave evidence of weight.

Some have suggested that Bigfoot and other anomalous creatures may have a sort of built-in camouflage that enables them to fool the human eye in a way that is very like the alien technology in *Predator*. Military science has reportedly made great strides in optical camouflage or invisibility technology—think Harry Potter's cloak adapted for use by soldiers—according to articles such as a May 15, 2008 post by the website, darkgovernment.com. One prototype that has already used nanotechnology to wrap electromagnetic waves around an object was demonstrated by Duke University physicist David R. Smith as early as 2006, in fact. But the hunter's encounter occurred about 30 years earlier.

If nothing else, this hunter's experience may show that the Bay area has a history of some type of unknown entity (for lack of a better word) in the vicinity of its old military range.

And wouldn't you know it; one other report from this area also involves something a shade beyond the physical.

Mrs. Wolf's Story

The married surname of the woman who reported this sighting really is Wolf, and she asked me to refer to her publicly as Mrs. Wolf. Her name, however, is more species-specific than was the actual creature that attacked her in her vehicle one night near Essexville in the late 1990s.

Essexville lies along Lake Huron just east of Bay City. Mrs. Wolf was then sixteen and living with her mother on a private drive off Jones Road, in a house that faced the bay. She was driving home from school in her mother's 1987 GMC Jimmy in mid-September at dusk, her mind full of the school play for which she had stayed late to audition. Her speed was no more than 45 miles per hour as she neared the intersection of Jones and Arms Roads, an irrigation ditch backed by trees and fields to the left of her and a shallow ditch and cornfield to the right. She passed through the intersection and drove just a bit farther when her side mirror revealed a large animal running alongside her truck. She slowed down and peered into the waning daylight as she tried to figure out what it was. She immediately discovered it was larger than a deer.

"It came up to about where the bottom of my window would be on the Jimmy," she said, "so (its back would have been) maybe four to four and one half feet. Its fur was shaggy and dark in color. It looked black, could have been a dark brown. It wasn't light like a deer's, that's for sure. It was rather bulky and ran on all fours, looked like heavy musculature though not as stocky as a bear. Its legs were also too long to be a bear."

About the time she realized that she could not identify the creature, it banged into the side of her truck, rocking it about a foot to the right. The creature still showed in the mirror, undaunted by its body hitting the moving vehicle. At that point, the young Mrs. Wolf-to-be stepped on the gas and rocketed the rest of the short way home, where she bolted into the house and locked all the doors, closed the blinds and lit every room before collapsing in frightened tears on the sofa. She was even too afraid to recount the whole story to her perplexed mother; she just said that "something" was out there.

Unfortunately for identification purposes, the creature ran with its head down, and she never got a good look at it. The body shape and the creature's behavior both seem to rule out a bear, and the dark shaggy fur makes a large cat unlikely. It sounds too large to be a goat, too tall for a wild boar. In my opinion, some type of canine fits the scenario best, right down to the car-chasing, which is also a trait reported by other manwolf witnesses from Doris Gipson on Bray Road to John Lyons of Reed City.

Mrs. Wolf did not observe the creature in an upright posture, either, so it is hard to rule this one a dogman. But it was certainly out of the ordinary.

She did tell me that she is a self-described "practitioner of the occult," that she saw a ghost when she was a child, and that at the age of thirteen, she once woke up in her room to see a pair of yellow eyes glowing at her and then heard something growl. She jumped up screaming and turned on the lights, but nothing was there.

This may have been what is known as a hypnopompic hallucination—an experience that can occur in the transition between sleep and waking (hallucinatory experiences when going to sleep are called hypnogogic). People may see, hear, smell and feel things—and often experience sleep paralysis at the same time. Mrs. Wolf insists she was fully awake, however, and was already sitting up. She was never able to shake the feeling that "something" was watching her whenever she went outside, right up to her truck encounter three years later.

Does Mrs. Wolf's history of paranormal experiences affect the validity of her sighting? In an effort to see whether such events make it more likely to see an anomalous creature, I often ask witnesses whether they have experienced anything in the paranormal realm. I would say it breaks down fifty-fifty between those who have and have not, and it does not seem to affect the type of sighting experienced by the witness. But Mrs. Wolf seemed to feel that the yellow eyes and the creature that loped along with her truck had some relation to one another, so I have included her thoughts for the reader's mulling pleasure.

The Farm Stalker

The next story from Iosco County really gave me the shivers. The writer, who requested the location be left out since they still live there, told it very well, so I have left the report in her words, with minor editing for spelling and punctuation:

"This happened on New Year's Eve of 2006-2007. My husband and children were down with colds, so all of them went to bed fairly early with cold medicines. I stayed up to do the nighttime chores. Right around twenty to midnight I decided to go get the outside chores done so that I could be done and come in to wake the kids to let them see the ball drop like we usually do.

"Nighttime chores consisted of letting in our Basset hounds for the night and putting out our two little mini-Dachshunds to their running pen one more time for the night. For us this New Year's Eve was warm, wet and soggy. It rained buckets the entire day long, stopping just around dark. It was chilly but certainly not freezing, so I slipped on my husband's big shoes and just ran out really quick in my nightgown like I usually did. This only took a couple of minutes anyway.

"Outside was so bright you could see everything, even out in the farmers field behind the house. Our yard is fenced and I always walk to the gate and take a look down the drive. Coyotes come in the yard and driveway nightly. When I was looking out the gate waiting for the dogs to finish running, I realized I had left the chicken coop door wide open. It has to be shut or the coyotes would clean out the chicken coop by morning. I didn't think anything of it. I don't mind, didn't mind being out at night. It was so bright from the moon I could see everything perfectly. I didn't need a flash light.

"The coop is a good way down our long driveway and has a row of pines along it just before the coop. That was the only part of the whole side yard that was in shadow, but I could still see. As I crossed the yard I noticed a fairly large, squarish object in front of the last pine, down on the ground. It made me stop walking for a minute. I just wanted to make sure that I wasn't walking up on an animal or something. I stared; it was solid black, never moved. I didn't pay any attention to the sick feeling I got; I thought it was just because I got startled and let myself get scared. I couldn't come back in and make my sick husband get up to go walk out in the wet and close the coup because I was scared.

"So I kept going. I decided to myself it was a hay bale in the shadow of the tree, standing on its end. (My boys practice archery shooting at hay bales and sometimes they move them about to different places in the yard.) I could see just fine, and was almost there when the black shape I had been staring at stood straight up. I say stood but it 'rose' up. Whatever it was had waited motionless until I was almost completely on top of it before it moved. It didn't lean forward or wobble and rock as is someone getting to their feet would. It simply rose up. It's the only word I can think of to use to describe it. Just effortlessly rose up. And what was already fairly tall sitting was extremely tall after standing.

"I was so close I could have tossed a rock and hit it if I could have moved. I have very bad panic reflexes I guess. I freeze and loose my voice completely. My husband has teased me of this since our dating years. But it's true. Especially when chased—even when I know it's just him. I couldn't move. And at first it just stood there facing off with me, neither one of us moving, and as bright as it was and as well as I could see. There was just solid blackness, no features at all. Just a shape. In my mind I was thinking I'm going to be kidnapped or murdered right here in my back yard, and nobody can hear me. But at the same time as my mind was racing around what was happening, I KNEW this wasn't a person. I just knew it, with no guessing. The top shape wasn't right.

"Our pause lasted only seconds, and then I seen it turn and walk (I say walked for lack of a better word) but it was not a walk. It went slowly and deliberately in a straight line right to the coop door (that I needed to get to and shut) and then turned around to face me again. My coop front is white lattice. So when it turned around I got a perfect look at his odd profile against the white of the chicken coop. It wasn't right. It wasn't a person.

"Later when I was telling my husband, I told him that it looked like the snout of a bear. And even though it took a few seconds and walked away from me a couple of yards I still could not make myself move. I stood there crying instead. When it turned around my feeling in my stomach turned from fear to just awful. I have never felt that way in the presence of anything ever. I completely believed whatever this was knew at that moment how terrified I was and that I could not run and it was enjoying every minute of having me trapped alone outside the gate.

"This took place all in not a few fleeting seconds but a few minutes. Possibly even five minutes or so. I finally got my feet to move, and I stumbled in my husband's big shoes a couple steps backwards. I had to go backwards because I couldn't take my eyes off of it. When I did this (move I mean), it left the coop and CROSSED the driveway to 'my' side of the yard. I never in the whole ordeal saw legs of any type animal or human. Just solid black. Strange head, no arm movements, ramrod straight and solid black all the way down. But he was coming now and I didn't know what to do. In my panic I couldn't focus on how quickly it was coming across the little gap between us.

"After tripping again over these shoes I was in I got out a single yell, as hard as I could. All I could get out between tears was NO! It stopped. It was so close, I was terrified and I kept thinking, if this wasn't really real it should have disappeared by now. But then as I took another step backward it continued again. If I dare moved it would move. But it went faster than me.

"I took another step back and it continued again. I managed a couple good strides to get closer to my gate. I looked over my shoulder, trying to keep my eyes on it, and it was about two car lengths away. I could 'feel' it if that makes any sense. I screamed 'NO!' again, and waved my arms and tried stomping these stupid shoes. It paused again, but as soon as I moved it would move. I was close enough now that I just bolted for my gate. As I ran through it and turned to look behind me, I seen the solid black shape back at the pines where it first was, and saw it move in between the pines and the coop and disappear. And that was that. I got the little dogs and myself in the house as fast as possible and ran inside and locked the door.

"When I came running in the door I woke up my husband who was on the couch. He knew something was wrong, but I wouldn't let him go outside. I kept trying to explain to him this wasn't a person of any sort. The next morning as soon as the sun came up he went out. Because of the all day rain, the clay and mud in the drive was so deep it pulled at your shoes. The driveway and all around the chicken coop were covered in coyote tracks. But then again, that isn't anything odd—it's a chicken coop and they come almost every night to see if I closed the coop. But then again I guess coyote tracks can be any size of dog track as well? I don't know. But no men's shoe prints in the deep mud. He could see where I was stuck in the mud and where I had turned around and gotten stuck again.

"I don't know, and I don't presume to know what this was. I know what it wasn't though. It wasn't a silent, upright walking bear that left no tracks. And it most surely wasn't a person of any sort of shape. I just know I will never be without that sickening feeling now being out the gate after dark. And I was always before comfortable roaming around the yard at night when I let the animals out for their last run. I will always remember that FIRST gut feeling I had that I ignored. I will listen to it next time no matter the consequence.

"As far as animals go, we are sandwiched in between a dairy farm and a sheep farm. Why something would sit and wait at my tiny coop of ten little chickens is beyond me. I had a feeling this something wasn't there for a chicken. It sat still as stone and waited for me.

"Now I had never heard of the dogman before. But I have heard tales of the Skin Walkers. But I must admit I never gave it much thought, and I believe that is a Navajo legend. I had at that time just before 2007 received some ceremonial feathers, for smudging and cleansing our house (and yard) from the Chief and Chief mother of the Southern Cherokee of Kentucky. They had sent me instructions on what to do and how to do it. It was more than just sage smudging. And after all of this event was said and done, I have went over it dozens of times in my head, and it was when I reached that smudge line, that this turned and left to where it came from. Whether that makes any sense or difference I don't know.

"Any animal could have reached me out there at any time in two good strides. This whatever-it-was left quickly as soon as I neared the gate. As soon as I entered the smudge line, ridiculous as it seems. I'm sure it wasn't me out there crying and tripping over my shoes in my pajamas that scared it away. Maybe I intrigued it because I didn't run away (because I couldn't), I don't know. But that's my story....

"That is when I started searching Google for strange happenings in and around Michigan, one snow day."

Creatures of the Upper Peninsula

Michigan's Upper Peninsula has a terrain and personality quite distinct from the southern part of the state. It is much less densely populated, still bearing some of the linguistic and cultural stamp left by the Finns who were among its most successful early settlers. With its wide swaths of forested wilderness and long, desolate stretches of Great Lakes shorelines, it would seem likely that the greatest share of Michigan sightings would be reported by Yoopers.

Not so.

Only a handful of creature reports have come to me from the U.P., versus dozens from the land of the "trolls"—the nickname Yoopers fondly bestow upon all those who live under (south of) the bridge at Sault Ste. Marie.

This may be partly due to the fact that there are simply fewer people there to encounter unknown creatures and more space in which the critters may hide. Or it may have to do with the U.P.'s harsh winters and deep snow levels that would make hunting much more difficult for any predator. The reports I do get tend to come from the more easily navigable and better populated perimeters of the U.P. I will share one from Iron Mountain, which is just across the Wisconsin/Michigan border, and another from the lakeside town of Gulliver. I have a few others, such as the 1997 daylight sighting of a hyena-like quadruped seen crossing Hwy. M-28 in the Hiawatha National Forest west of Sault Ste. Marie, but they don't quite make the cut.

The first one I'll tell is not the strongest story I've heard, either. The writer told of an experience his father had when a Boy Scout at a camp somewhere in the region of Iron Mountain (possibly the now private Northwoods Scout Reservation near Watersmeet, which is also near the Wisconsin border and near the famous Paulding "spook" lights).

He didn't know exactly what year it occurred, but it was sometime in the early 1960s. The story goes that one of the Scouts woke up during the night and saw the outline of a wolf walking on its hind legs cast on the wall of his tent by the firelight outside. He yelled, and the creature emitted a piercing shriek as it ran off into the darkness.

I would chalk this up to an ordinary campfire tale, and it probably is just that, but I do think it's worth noting that this was over twenty years before the Michigan Dogman legend became widely known. If it was a prank, it was unusually original.

The Gulliver incident is a bit meatier. It was actually sent first to the Michigan-dogman.com site operated for several years by Steve Cook. And like the Boy Scout Camp kerfuffle, it occurred in the 1960s-1968, to be exact.

The writer was thirteen, he said, when he caught sight of an animal he described as "a cross between a wolverine and a man or ape." It was a late, fall afternoon, and he was headed to the cow barn for chores when he noticed the cows sounded disturbed over something, which was unusual at that time of day.

As he opened the barn door to investigate, he heard something growl at him from a darkened corner. Immediately terrified, he picked up a pitchfork for self-defense, ducked back out and ran for the house. Before he got there, he saw the creature he assumed had growled at him, running on two legs "like a man" through the field behind the barn. It was covered with dark brown fur with a lighter brown area over its shoulder area, and he estimated its height at six feet. It had a brushy tail, and the writer thought he saw a large snout but didn't have a good look at the face. He was sure it wasn't a bear.

The animal continued on its hind legs for at least fifty yards, then dropped to all fours before bounding into the woods. He never saw it again. When his father went to the barn later, however, he discovered torn bales of hay. Neighbors told of finding animal carcasses eaten and buried near their property, and one man said he had seen a "wolfman" near the writer's farm. The family even contacted the Michigan DNR but received no response.

I find this second story quite compelling and very much in line with incidents reported on other farms around the country. But all in all, these two lone incidents do not make a good showing for such a large chunk of terrain that certainly teems with other wildlife. Perhaps the dogman really doesn't care for deep snow. Maybe Yoopers are not aware that I'm recording reports. Or it could be that the residents of the U.P. are simply very good at keeping the old secrets of their hardscrabble peninsula.

PART TWO

Werewolves West of the Mississippi

One misconception that often rears its bristly head during radio shows or other forums is that creatures like the Beast of Bray Road or the Michigan Dogman are unique to Wisconsin and Michigan and that they remain curiously absent in the rest of the continent and world. The truth is that sightings of bipedal, oddly-behaving canines or lupines occur in a wide variety of locations, terrains, and geographical settings around this planet, including occasional forays into urban areas.

Within the mass of these reports, I do notice trends, hotspots, and concentrations along certain lake and river corridors or near some wildlife areas—he Manistee National Forest, for example—that suggest to me that these creatures may migrate with the seasons or to stake out new territory. This is common behavior among other predatory mammals such as gray wolves or cougars, so it should not be unexpected that manwolves or dogmen would do the same if they are indeed flesh-and-blood animals.

And if upright canines are manifestations of earth spirits or various religious cultures, then they would appear wherever attuned humans go—otherwise, no one would be observing and reporting them. No surprise there either.

It's interesting to me that there are far more sightings east of the Mississippi River than west of it, and yet I have received a pile of reports from the western half of the country since *Hunting the American Werewolf* was published. This collection feels like fresh meat, so let's have a look on the other side of what Algonquian-speaking peoples called "Big River" before proceeding with the more populous eastern states.

I will start with Oklahoma, the state of Okies, mountains, plains and panhandle. The Canadian River meanders through it, and the eastern side of the state is well-watered with the Oologah, Cherokee and Eufalah Lake systems. It sounds like a perfect place for creatures of all kinds to hide. My earliest reported sighting goes back to the early 1980s.

Chapter 6

Oklahoma Beasts: Atoka to Antlers

The time was one in the morning and it was a clear autumn night in 1981 as two men in their twenties sped along Highway 3 heading northwest between Atoka and Antlers, passing the McGee Creek Lake and State Forest on their way to Stillwater. Their 1972 Ford Maverick cruised under dark skies illuminated by a thin slice of moonlight, with farm fields adjacent to both sides of the road. The person that wrote me, now in his fifties, estimates they were about five miles from the Muddy Boggy Bridge, a historic through-truss bridge built in 1933 over the Muddy Boggy River, when they spotted the creature on the highway's right shoulder. The writer added that neither he nor his friend had been drinking.

"It was just standing still with no movement…very close to the line that defines the lane for cars. It was absolutely on two legs. I thought it was a tall man when the headlights first hit it. I didn't notice (anything) from the knees down, but from the knees up to the jaw line it looked very much like a very athletic male."

He added that the creature seemed about seven feet tall, with a weight of whatever an Olympic gymnast of that height (if there are any gymnasts that tall) might be. It was covered with very short, "absolutely black" fur, and he could not see its paws.

"The arm was hanging at its side," he said, "and the lower details disappeared in the silhouette. One of the strange things was how the light didn't reflect and light up the silhouette to show more detail. Shape is what I remember."

He compared that shape to Anubis, Egyptian jackal-or-dog-headed god of the dead. Readers of *Hunting the American Werewolf* will remember hearing that same comparison from the witnesses of a creature spotted at the Great Lakes Naval Base north of Chicago in September, 1994.

"The head had a human shape except for two very distinct features. The ears were like a wolf's, but smaller. The nose and mouth was like a Malamute...again very much like a wolf but smaller."

The man's first thought was that it was a human who was either drunk or playing a dangerous prank, until his car drew closer. When he was only about ten feet away from it, the creature stepped right in front of the speeding Maverick and ran very quickly across the road on two legs, never glancing at the two men in their car. The men were totally stunned when the creature reached the other side of the road and dropped to all fours to enter the field without breaking speed or stride.

"It never turned to look at us but seemed very intent on something in the field across the road," he said. "Never saw the eyes. Certainly nothing red and glowing. Never saw teeth or claws."

The man said he may have glimpsed a tail, but wasn't sure.

"I kept expecting to see or notice something that would explain rationally what I was seeing, but (its) crossing in front of the car and how it was low (under four feet tall) on all fours as it moved into the field removed rational explanations. Fear verging on terror was the immediate aftermath. I didn't look out the window or in the rearview mirror for fear of seeing something keeping pace with the car."

The man stepped on the gas pedal, sped up from sixty mph to seventy-five, and kept it there. His friend noticed and remarked that the car had picked up speed, and the man affirmed that it had. The friend said, "Go faster." They did not feel safe until after they had crossed the Muddy Boggy Creek Bridge, and they did not speak again until they reached Ada.

Safely within the city's limits, his friend finally dared to ask the writer why he stepped on the gas. He replied, "Same reason you wanted me to drive even faster." His friend said nothing and would reply only, "Maybe," when pressed as to whether he had also seen the creature.

The thought of returning to look for footprints never occurred to either of them, and the man says he has been back to the area only once in thirty years—and would not venture on that stretch of highway again except at high noon with a large group of people. While he and his friend wish to remain anonymous to the public, he said that he would be willing to take a lie detector test or even sodium pentathol if it would help people to believe him!

This creature sounds a bit atypical for a manwolf with its sleek, black fur, shorter muzzle, and smaller pointed ears on top of its head. Besides the Anubis reference, it also reminds me of a very similar creature seen by witnesses in California and in Eau Claire, Wisconsin, that manifested supernatural qualities such as the ability to appear within a house. But there is an unrelated sighting of another black-furred canine in this state to consider.

Terror in a Toyota

Fast forward twelve years to 1993 in Okarche, a small town about twenty-five miles northwest of Oklahoma City, set in the central portion of the state. A young, married man named Brandon had driven with a friend in his small Toyota to a secluded dirt road five miles east of town just to get away and unwind. They parked the car, rolled down the windows and proceeded to complain about their lives as young (and old) people do, when they heard a strange noise coming from some tall weeds just off the road.

"As quickly as I heard the noise," he wrote, "this thing was right up in my face. I was so scared my breath went out of me. I only had time to look in its eyes as it looked back at me."

As the pair stared at one another, the creature turned its head to glare head on with eyes that glowed red. "I felt that it looked through me, not just at me." He described it as huge, at least seven feet tall, as it bent to put its head at window level.

"It was black with a very furry head and pointed erect ears. It had its mouth part open showing me its teeth. They were that of a massive canine. I didn't smell anything, but I think that there wasn't enough time for that to register. It was heavy enough that when it put its claws or paws on the top and bottom of my window that it actually shook the car."

He panicked, and tried to move from the driver's seat to to climb over his friend in the passenger seat to get away—but was restrained by his seatbelt. He was certain the creature would bite off his left shoulder and pull him from the vehicle, but nothing happened.

"I fully expected its mouth to cover my entire shoulder. I mean entire shoulder blade to mid-chest. That's how big its mouth was. It was very menacing." When he turned slowly to look out the window, the beast was gone. It was not visible in the side mirror, either. By then he was shaking so hard that his passenger had to insert the keys into the ignition so they could skedaddle.

"When we were pulling away, I was asking my friend, 'Do you see it? Do you see it?'" He only heard it rush the car and felt the car move when it put its claws on it. He was freaking out from my behavior. I was expecting this thing to chase us and wasn't comfortable until we were several miles away and over seventy mph. I want to say I checked the car for marks but I'm not sure.

"To this day I can't go in the country anymore, especially at night. I only told a couple of people about it, and I don't think they believed me. The only description that has ever made sense to me is a werewolf. Less than a mile from where this happened is a feedlot where there are literally thousands of cattle. I know from the size of this thing that it could have killed me quickly if it wanted to.

"I could tell from its eyes that there was intelligence. There wasn't an animal's soul in there. I think it was trying to scare us away. It sure worked. I've thought about this almost every day since and haven't been able to find anything close to logical closure. I have four kids and watch them closer than most parents because I know the world has something out there that isn't normal. And if there's one then there's more elsewhere. I know you're looking for these things in your quest. Believe me, you don't want to find one."

Okay. Gulp. Brandon's story is frightening because of the creature's close proximity and the possibility that it could have done him real harm. And yet, these manwolves never do. I also thought it was striking that, like the man in the last report, he had a strange fear that the creature would chase him. Also, both men seemed deeply affected by their experiences, to the point that they took care not to place themselves where a repeat performance was likely. I think, too, that knowledge of the nearby giant cattle lot adds a motive for the creature to have lurked in that area.

My third Oklahoma close encounter again involved two people driving at night.

Tree-Hugger Wolfman

The about-to-be-witnesses were driving home around 11:00 p.m. along a back road in Foyil in northeast Oklahoma one summer evening in 1998, when the driver suddenly swerved. Just in time, he had spied something six to seven feet tall with brown fur holding onto a tree and leaning forward—as if it was about to jump in front of their vehicle. Its eyes glowed bright yellow in the headlights.

They just missed hitting it, and kept driving in a state of near panic. The person who wrote to me, the driver, was sure it was not a bear.

Foyil, I might add, is only a few miles east of Oologah Lake, with 29,500 acres of water and many public hunting areas for a variety of game, making it a very reasonable habitat.

The Other Side of Oologah

Another incident happened recently, only a quick swim and short run west of the Foyil sighting.

US Hwy 60 runs right over the lake's northern tip, and a couple wrote me that they were driving east on that highway about 1:30 a.m. on a bright, moonlit night in early November, 2009, between Pawhuska and Bartlesville when they noticed a large creature hunched over a deer carcass on the north side of the road. The husband slowed down for a better look as he and his wife craned their necks to stare in disbelief.

The creature was "squatting in what looked like a three-point lineman's stance eating the deer. It was very large, between six and seven feet tall," he wrote. "With a muscular build. Its legs were thick and covered in black hair, and its arms were long and muscular. I didn't get a clear look at its face outside of the fact it had an elongated snout and reddish eyes."

When they realized they could not identify the giant beast, the man and his wife sped up to escape it. But that was not the end of this story.

"I must have angered it," he said, "because it started running after us. It jumped across the highway to the southern side (which I was driving on) and gave chase." They soon outdistanced the creature and kept going.

"The whole rest of the way we tried to work out what we saw," he said. "There is nothing that we can think of that fits what we saw. No coyote or mountain lion I've ever seen has been as large as what I've seen. I don't drink and I don't use drugs. I wasn't tired as I had slept till about five in the afternoon that day."

While this man did not mention seeing the creature run bipedally, the "three-point stance" is certainly unusual, as are the red eyeshine, the large size and the long limbs. The creature hunching over a deer carcass and chasing the vehicle certainly are features of a classic sighting. Adding it to the many other accounts of people flooring the gas pedal upon seeing these things, it makes me wonder how many have been stopped for speeding and admitted to the officer they were fleeing from a werewolf.

Boogerman or Skinwalker? Trickster Meets Trickster

That eastern part of Oklahoma seems to be a sort of creature corral. I received an extensive set of emails from Joe, a military veteran who grew up south of Muskogee on Eufala Lake.

Joe, a middle-aged man who has earned several advanced degrees and is very active in his community, started off by admitting something unusual. As a tall teenager with very large feet, he loved to leap around barefoot in the mud and sand in camping areas to leave "Bigfoot" prints for others to find. He also would come back at night and blow into a hunting horn to make a bellowing, hooting sound, and even went so far as to scare people on hiking and biking trails by wearing a mask and fake fur coat and then jumping out as they approached. He would try to appear surprised and then let out a big roar and chase them for a short distance.

These events occurred in the 1970s, and he estimates he scared about five different people this way over several years. The pranks embarrass him now, especially after he began to have his own experiences.

The first occurred when he was only fifteen. While alone in the woods one day, he froze when he heard a deep-throated yell that he knew was not a hunting horn, a bobcat, or any other animal he had ever heard on his treks through the forests near his home. A Native American neighbor told him the sound was made by a Skinwalker, and that her brother had encountered a four-foot tall, fur-covered humanoid around 1920 in those same forests. It had a long snout, light-colored eyes and acted menacing and angry, she said, and it shot up a tree and emitted a scream similar to the one Joe had described.

She further explained the nature of Skinwalkers, a type of magical creature common to the lore of many North American indigenous people to him:

"They described them as being evil forest spirits, not as big as humans but just as strong, and also cunning and very malicious. The Skinwalkers are supposed to be masters of camouflage, their dark coloration and long fur/hair allow them to hide in the shadows under the trees very effectively, plus they have a tendency to only come out at night. The Skinwalkers supposedly hate humans and will try to kill them if they can.

"Usually they target young children, luring them…by mimicking the sound of a kitten or puppy, or sometimes mimicking the sound of kids laughing. If a Skinwalker can get a young child alone in the woods, they will strangle them. Another tactic is to get older children or even small adults alone and into water like a creek or pond. Then the Skinwalkers will spring upon the victim and hold them underwater and drown them. The lady said her parents warned them that if they ever see a shadow move independently, you must keep your eyes down and pretend you didn't notice and leave the area quickly."

Joe said that as he grew older and researched the topic, he was unsure whether the neighbor used the right term, since Skinwalkers are usually considered by the Navajo and other southwestern US Native Americans to be larger manifestations created by malevolent human shamans. I would agree with his conclusion, but it is still a startling story.

Joe and those close to him would have later encounters between August and November, 2006, in an area forty-five miles southeast of Oklahoma City, in a partially wooded area of farms and brushy fields and grasslands where he hunted and fished. The experiences ranged from a sense of being watched to his girlfriend seeing something large, dark and growling coming at her through the cattails as she stood and fished, to his hunting partner seeing a 200-pound black "wolf" with disproportionately large head, shoulders and torso beneath his tree stand. The hunter told Joe the creature was stalking him on all fours but moving more as a human would do. Joe said his friend is not the type to panic but was pale and shaking after the incident.

As much as I appreciated Joe's sharing of his story, I had to tell him that some might think his admitted youthful pranks cloud his credibility a bit. He replied that he had nothing to gain by telling me his experiences, and indeed I think that if he were still playing tricks he would probably have come up with something a little more sensational. His story does drive home the need to always keep the possibility of hoaxes in mind.

Manwolves of Muskogee

I'm glad that at least one eastern Oklahoman report comes from the town with my favorite Okie name: Muskogee. The report stemmed from multiple sightings of wolf-like creatures by the brother-in-law of a woman who wrote after hearing me on *Coast to Coast AM* radio. The brother-in-law agreed to let her interview him as long as his name wasn't given, and she wrote up a thorough account for me. I will call him Ed.

Ed's first initiation into the world of cryptid canines came one night as he took the Chandler Road ramp to get on the Muskogee Turnpike to Tulsa late one night early in 2006. As he entered the on-ramp, he noticed a gray wolf devouring a deer. The wolf stared at him with what he described as "intelligent eyes," and it made Ed feel very unsettled.

That in itself would not be so odd, but a few days later his fiancée saw another wolf eating a deer on the same ramp. This one was black, however, and was eating like a human would, by using its front paw to put food in its mouth. More than merely unsettled by the sight, she felt this creature exuded "evil."

Three years later, in July, 2009, they saw a large gray wolf while driving to a rented storage unit. It was on all fours but was so large they estimated it would stand seven feet tall on its hind legs. The wolf was just ahead of them on the roadside, and it wove in and out of the nearby tree line as it kept pace for about one-eighth mile, until they came to a church with a sign in front. To their extreme shock, the wolf was perched atop the church's sign, fifteen feet off the ground! There were no trees or other objects near the sign that would have provided a climbing surface, and yet the creature sat there staring down at them as they passed.

In March of 2009, the black wolf showed itself to yet another family member, the writer's mother-in-law, on the very same ramp where it and the gray wolf had been seen before. She and a friend, who was driving, both saw the very large, dark animal's eyes glow red. The friend started to slow down as the mother-in-law screamed for her to keep going and to lock the doors, which she finally did. The friend later said she felt the "dog was in her head and that it was telling her it was a nice dog and she should stop to rescue it." It was probably best for them that they did not.

This very odd cluster of sightings reminds me of an incident from *Hunting the American Werewolf*, where three young women saw what they thought was an abandoned dog on a ramp to Interstate 94 in Brookfield, Wisconsin in December, 2000. Like the Muskogee woman, they also felt they should stop and rescue it, but they were deterred when it stood up and ran off on its hind legs toward a nearby, deserted golf course.

These incidents make me wonder whether off-on ramps are the new version of traditional crossroads, which have long been known in almost every culture as the haunts of malign spirits. Author and researcher Paul Devereaux wrote in his book, *Haunted Land*, that "as well as deities, all the supernatural creatures of the night were associated with crossroads." He added that "crossroads were special haunts of the traveling spirits of ecstatic witches and werewolves…" and goes on to document his belief that even ordinary roadways in our physical world may be places where the spirit realms intermingle with our own.

This brings me to my second thought, related to the wolf on the church sign, that there is a very similar body of folklore regarding churchyards and phantom canines. Great Britain is particularly rich in these tales, which can also involve other animals such as black cats or black pigs.

These Muskogee creatures certainly have an otherworldly quality, with the red eyes, hand-to-mouth bad table manners and the weird church sign-sitting. This would not be unheard of in Oklahoma. The area around Ada in southern central Oklahoma has long been rumored to be haunted by werewolves, but the legend is based on a 1917 tombstone in Kanawa. It belongs to a young woman killed in her late teens and reads, "Killed by human wolves." Historians are clear that these "wolves" were two local men, a doctor and a schoolteacher, who also killed another young woman. Oklahoma author Steven E. Wedel wrote a novel about the incident and named it after the inscription.

As another historical side note, I found another, older Oklahoma incident in "1971 Humanoid Reports" on Albert Rosales' UFOinfo.com site. It occurred in Lawton, Oklahoma after dark in February 1971 at the home of Jackie and Ron Dee. When Jackie made a quick trip to retrieve some items from the couple's back porch, she saw what she described as a fur-covered humanoid with a wolf-like face staring at her from the back yard. She screamed for Ron, and the two of them watched the creature vault over a fence as it emitted a loud and threatening growl. Lawton is in the southwest section of the state, about thirty miles north of the Texas border (and too far from Eufala Lake for the incident to be credited to former hoaxer Joe, above).

As a final note, other witnesses have also sometimes felt the creature was sending them a message of some sort, usually along the lines of "stay there" or "you can't get me." The suggestion to "stop and rescue me" is the scariest I've heard.

Beast on the Border

One last sighting in this chapter actually occurred just over the border in Siloam Springs, Arkansas, but since it is within a mile or so of northeastern Oklahoma I think it fits better here.

The report came in February, 2008, from a woman whose fiancé had an encounter one night in 2004-2005 while driving through Siloam Springs (on US Hwy 412, I presume). There was a full moon and clear viewing conditions.

The man, who is Native American, was about to go over a bypass above some railroad tracks when he spotted a creature "with a head like a Doberman and pointy ears."

The woman wrote, "Its arms were curled up and next to its body. He recalls its legs reminded him of a deer but he could have just thought that since it was running upright. He said it jumped over the safety rails on one side of the road, took about three steps, and jumped over the rails on the other side of the four-lane highway. It was fast."

Her fiancé naturally wondered what the creature was, so he turned back as soon as he could and returned to the area by the tracks, but the animal had disappeared by then.

"There was a car behind him and a car coming over the bypass, which he thought had to have seen it. We were both raised in this area but have never heard of anything like this. He says it did remind him of the picture you see of the ancient Egyptians of the dog creatures. He was also an avid hunter, so his eye is always open for deer. This time he got more than he expected. We are both Native American and have heard of shapeshifting, but nothing about anything like this."

Chapter 7

More Western Wild Things

Dog-Faced People of Mississippi

Famed European merchant explorer Marco Polo claimed that he encountered dog-headed people, or Cynocephali, in his travels around Asia in the late 1200s. I also ran across several references to Native American "dog-faced" people called *Hattak Ofi*, or "man-dog," in Oklahoma. A story of a similar creature came from a Cherokee man in Mississippi, who told me about the *Hattak Chito*, or "big man," a creature of swamps and marshes that looks like a large, fur-covered human and normally avoids people. Most people would interpret that description as akin to a Bigfoot.

But what this next man saw February 6, 2009, in Prentiss County, looked like a classic dogman. That is notable considering the area's ancient tradition among indigenous people as a Sasquatch habitat. If he had any expectations of seeing an anomalous creature on his hike through the woods that bright morning, it would logically have been something that looked more like Bigfoot. Indeed, one often-cited skeptical response to creature sightings is that people are merely seeing what they expect to see, filling in the blanks in their mind to turn, say, a deer into a Bigfoot. But that is not what happened in this case.

Bryan Wallin, a researcher and co-host of the Blogtalk Radio show *Nite Callers*, had taken a folding camping chair on a short hike into a hardwood forest to spend some time in an outdoor setting. With a lifelong interest in the *Hattak Chito*, he did hope that a Bigfoot might come into view if he sat quietly and waited.

He had walked and stopped several times when he decided to sit and observe a small group of cedar trees between 150 and 200 feet away from him. He had just seated himself when he noticed something dark brown or black lurking beneath one large cedar with long, drooping branches.

The "thing" did not notice him because it was intently focused on something else, crouched in a "three-point" stance with legs flexed at what looked like the knee; the tree branches prevented a clear look at more of the body or the feet and front paws, although the shoulder was visible. Finally, it turned its head, and Wallin was shocked to see that its profile was that of a German shepherd with a long, canine snout.

"That is when this wave of extreme terror came over me," he wrote. "I was completely stunned and very frightened that this thing might come toward me."

He began to think about the twelve-inch hunting knife—his only means of protection—as he slowly rose from his seat, picked it up and began to back out of the vicinity, trying to avoid snapping twigs or otherwise drawing attention to himself. He managed to get back to his car in this way and immediately lit out for home.

"When I got home I was still trembling, and it took the better part of a day for me to calm down," Wallin wrote. "I did not sleep well at all that night and had recurring dreams of this for a couple of days. I only went to this area to look for Sasquatch signs, i.e., footprints, limb breaks and formations, never in my wildest dreams thinking I would see anything like this."

North Dakota Dogman

Fargo, North Dakota is better known as the site of the quirky Coen Brothers movie of the same name than as a place of cryptozoological weirdness, yet I received a very believable report of an incident that occured in a Fargo neighborhood a few miles from the Red River in 1997. The twenty-three-year-old woman who reported it in July, 2009, was only eleven at the time of a frighteningly close encounter that has haunted her through the years.

There was a flood in Fargo that year, and she and her friends spent a lot of time playing in the muddy ditches in her area. One of their favorite games was a version of hide-and-seek they called Ghost in the Graveyard. She and a friend were hiding in a ditch partly filled with water, as another friend sat up in a tree and another, playing the part of the ghost, walked around. The others got up to run for the base and so did the writer, but before she could leave the ditch she heard a noise behind her. She knew that about fifty yards of open ground, bordered by a tree line deemed out-of-bounds, lay in that direction—and wondered why any of her friends would have run that way.

They hadn't. But she continued to hear what sounded like a person walking through crunchy leaves and twigs. She could hear her friends arguing in the opposite direction so she knew it was not one of them. As she tried to decide what to do, the crunching finally stopped. She turned to peer into the darkness toward the tree line and heard a low growl, "like it didn't want to be heard or was trying to decide what I was or if I was a threat."

The creature stood much taller than her on its hind legs, she said, "but it had bad posture or wasn't too sure of standing upright. It was hairy all over and had a face similar to a husky's. It was dark-colored."

Its eyes were almond-shaped, and it moved its head from side to side as it studied her. She doesn't remember any odor other than the smell of the damp earth. She estimates they stared at one another for around forty–five seconds before the creature made a move as if to step closer, stretching one "hand" toward her.

"It looked like a deformed wolf paw," she said, but with very long claws. At that point she leaped out of the ditch and ran as fast as she could to where her friends were, not daring to look back to see whether it was chasing her. She lied to her friends about what had scared her so badly, telling them it was a crazy person who lived on the street.

She said that she tried to convince herself that it was a bear or a human, but added she knows what a bear looks like and that a human does not have dog legs and can't move the way this animal did. She went back to the ditch the next day with her own pet dog, but it only wanted to run home. She still shudders to think what could have happened had the creature decided to pursue her and wonders why her flight did not trigger its canine instinct to the chase.

One other communication I received from North Dakota in 2008 was a "tip" that werewolves were living in the sewers of Minot. My husband, who is a civil engineer specializing in wastewater management, confirmed that coyotes or other large mammals can sometimes invade certain types of underground wastewater systems, but that is the closest I've come to corroborating that tip in any way. I can see, however, why any creature might want to get underground in a North Dakota winter.

Chapter 8

Texas Terribles

From time to time, especially in the southern states, I will hear about a weird hybrid beast some call a "snout-nosed" Bigfoot. It sounds like a cross between dogman and man-ape, which is not genetically feasible. A few writers have defended that concept by saying that baboons have facial features—snout, fangs and visible ears—that resemble those of canids, so why not assume Old Snoutnose is just some variant of Bigfoot? The trouble with this notion is that Bigfoot, as usually described, is very much a member of the great ape family. Baboons are not apes but Old World monkeys of Africa and Asia, therefore genetically incompatible with any great ape. If there are indeed anomalous baboons infesting our wild areas, we then have three different types of unknown creatures to contend with: great ape, great canid and great Old World monkey.

Besides, baboons do not really fit most sighting reports of either Manwolf or Bigfoot. Their bodies max out at about forty inches in length, so they would not stand six to seven feet tall. They normally walk on all fours, although they will wade through deep water bipedally, and their long, thin tails and bare, prominent rumps are unmistakable features that I never hear mentioned in reports of either dogman or Bigfoot.

Others have proposed that all manwolf sightings are misidentified, escaped baboons. It is entirely possible that this could be the case in a few instances where quadrupeds have been glimpsed from a distance or partially obscured by weather or landscape, but there would have to have been hundreds of escaped, oversized bipedal baboons running amok over the whole country for many decades for this idea to work as a blanket solution.

Back to Texas.

Giant Rusty Bab-coon?

While we are talking baboons, one man who has lived in several southern states wrote to say that he had spotted what appeared to be Giant Rusty Baboons as well as Bigfoot-like skunk apes in many states as well as Texas. He is a Native American who uses a bicycle to commute to work, and while riding one night on Shoal Creek Boulevard on the northwest side of Austin, he spotted what first appeared to be a raccoon under a streetlight. On closer inspection, it looked much like a juvenile baboon on all fours—except it had no tail and its body shape was wrong and its hind legs were too long. Those are a lot of "excepts."

It studied him from about ten feet away as the man stopped his bike to stare back, observing its reddish fur, short snout, giant canine teeth and baboon-like hands and feet. He estimated its weight at thirty to forty pounds. (Full-grown male baboons will weigh thirty to eighty pounds depending on species.) The creature then "bounded" away into an adjacent wildlife area on all fours. The man rode off in complete puzzlement.

He continued to use that same commuter route, and a short time later encountered the creature again. This time the creature squatted as the two watched each other, the man using a light on his bike helmet for illumination. A low-pitched hissing sound from the darkness nearby made both of them swivel their heads, and the man gasped as his helmet light revealed a full-grown, obviously nursing female of the same species that, according to later measurements of a tree adjacent to her position, stood nine feet tall. He estimated her weight at 1,000 pounds, about 700 pounds more than the greatest manwolf weight estimate any witness has ever made.

She appeared completely and naturally bipedal as she "raised her right hand to block the bright light from her eyes and said something a bit louder to Junior who immediately bolted toward her at a sprint." Neither creature's eyes reflected eyeshine.

The two creatures then ran off into the darkness.

The man returned the next day to measure the sapling where the mother beast had stood and to look for footprints and hair. The ground was too hard and dry for prints, he said, but he did detect a musty, bad-smelling odor on area vegetation, although he did not mention noticing any smell during his encounter. I asked for a sketch via email but received no response. He did not give a date other than to say it occurred "several years" earlier. Since his email arrived in May, 2008, I will assume he meant the early-to-mid-2000s.

The man wondered in his letter if these snout-nosed creatures could be the source of werewolf legends, but they sound much larger and different than the usual long-muzzled, pointy-eared, canid-footed, bushy-tailed manwolf so many people have reported. And they sound very much different than eastern Texas' native red wolf, which weighs only up to 80 pounds at very most and whose snout is longer than a timber wolf's.

Might this be another type of large, unknown primate? Do anomalous, huge great apes compete with anomalous great monkeys in Texas and other southern states? Perhaps, if these witness accounts are to be believed. I just don't think they can explain away all reports of dogmen.

Austin Anomaly

Austin was also the location of another sighting within the same general timeline as the above incident. This one was made by a Las Vegas graphic artist named Josh, whose employer sent him on a business trip to Austin in summer, 2000, when he was twenty-one. He was driving back to Vegas at about 4:30 a.m. at about 45 mph along US 290, just southwest of the city, when he noticed an animal barely out of headlight range running along a deer fence on the side of the highway. The animal appeared to be running at the same pace as his car. He assumed it was a very fast deer, until it broke right through the fence and ran onto the highway in front of his vehicle on two legs.

"What I saw was about five feet tall. I remember brown and white fur along the chest and back area. The legs were more wolf-like than anything human."

Its head also resembled a wolf's, although its snout was a bit shorter, he said, and the eyes reflected brightly in his headlights as they made contact with his own. He could see a canine-like tongue and teeth in the open mouth, and felt that he had a very complete look at the creature. He did not notice a tail, but if the creature was upright, the tail may have been held close to its body.

The creature crossed the road and tore through the fence on that side, and Josh pulled over. "Then this is very stupid," he wrote, "but I got out of the car. I would not have dared to do this now. I swear to you I heard a wolf howl. I jumped back in my car and drove off at a very high speed. I have never used that route since that incident."

Josh said he believes the creature he saw was a mutation of some animal that resembled a werewolf. As he described it, it sounds much smaller and more canine than the nine-foot beast examined by the previous witness, but both were furry, bipedal creatures with snouts and were spotted on the western, more watered side of Austin, within a time frame of about five years or less. It appears something odd is going on within Austin's watershed and greenbelt areas.

UFOinfo.com also features a March, 1988, report from Brownfield in Hockley County, southwest of Lubbock, wherein a person driving north on FR173 saw a man-sized, bipedal creature with canine legs cross the highway just ahead of her. It had black fur and walked slightly hunched at the neck, as manwolves are usually reported to do. Its eyes reflected red in the headlights. The writer claimed Brownfield had a local history of similar sightings.

Beastly Biped of Sanger

The little town of Sanger sits sixty miles north of Dallas, not far from the Oklahoma border. In October, 1985, on a clear, warm night around 1:00 a.m., a young man saw a bipedal, hairy, five-foot-tall creature walking along a road west of town. He told his brother Chuck, who asked if it might have been a Sasquatch, but the brother replied that it was not because it had a wolf's face and snout. Its hair or fur was light brown, and its eyes reflected a greenish color in the lights of the young man's pickup truck.

The creature was just stepping out on the road near an old iron bridge and a wooded area when the brother's lights hit it. It paused, then stepped back into the high grass of the ditch.

Chuck wrote me in November, 2005, but said his brother still remembered the incident very well.

Texas does have a history of werewolf-like creatures. Mrs. Delburt Gregg reported seeing one claw at her window in 1958 in eastern Gregg County, near Longview in eastern Texas, in a story that appeared in *FATE Magazine*. In *Hunting the American Werewolf*, I mentioned the San Antonio area legend of the Converse Carnivore. This story from the *San Antonio Express-News Sunday Magazine*, October 29, 1989, involved a thirteen-year-old boy who claimed a werewolf-like creature was stalking him as he hunted with a group in the 1960s. No one believed him, so he returned to his hunting station alone. A mounted search party later found the wolfen creature devouring the boy's corpse. Researcher and author Nick Redfern, who makes his home in the Lone Star State, has written about werewolf sightings there, as well as in his native Great Britain's Cannock Chase.

Southwest Highways Dog-Like Thing, Chupy and Coyote Man

The stretch of highway on New Mexico's Interstate 25 between Fort Bliss and Albuquerque normally provides an uneventful ride. A man named Antonio experienced anything but that the night of May 16, 2008, as he passed near Las Cruces at about 75 mph.

"To my left I saw something that caught my attention," he wrote. "There was road kill on the side of the road and standing over it was this BIG dog-like thing. It was HUGE! About 170 pounds. It was definitely canid. It had shaggy brown fur, a long muzzle and pointy ears on top of its head. Its eyes glowed red when my headlights hit the thing. Honestly, I was scared."

Antonio said that although he needed to use a bathroom, and at the time was only a mile from a rest stop, he was too scared to do anything but plow on until he reached his destination in Albuquerque. He added that he had to pass through an immigration checkpoint after only a few miles, and the officials there seemed concerned due to his freaked out demeanor.

Antonio is an infantry soldier trained in close combat, he said, but not even his service in Iraq frightened him as much as seeing this creature. He added that he was not drinking, and that drugs were out of the question given his position with the military. Antonio did admit, however, that he was "involved" with supernatural activities all through high school, including such practices as summoning demons. He believes that he was able to summon a "spirit guardian" once and that it manifested as a white wolf.

"But," he added, "werewolves or monster wolves are not really part of any magical tradition I was affiliated with. I have always believed that werewolves are fictional, not saying what I saw was a werewolf but I know it was something, for the fact that it scared the crap out of me."

This part of the country also has a reputation for other cryptids. My husband and I were on vacation in Arizona a few years ago and met a real estate saleswoman who told us she saw what she thought was a *chupacabras*, or "goat-sucker," along Hwy 10 between Las Cruces and Tucson, almost directly west of Antonio's sighting, several years earlier than his incident. It was also standing upright, but had bat-like wings. Descriptions of *chupacabras*, a cryptid reported most often in Latin parts of the Americas, especially Puerto Rico, vary widely but usually come down to something about the size and shape of a kangaroo with dorsal spikes and sometimes wings.

Does this mean the manwolves and *chupacabras* are related? Not at all, but as I have noted in my other books, where one weird thing shows up, others often follow. And I have another strange sighting from Interstate 10 in Arizona that took place in 1976 at 2:00 a.m. about fifty miles west of Phoenix. Roger, the man who wrote, was riding in the back seat and trying to sleep as his two friends drove and chatted up front. Suddenly, he said, he was rudely awakened as they both began shouting, "What was that?" Both of his friends, natives of that desert landscape, both described seeing a short creature waddling on two legs along the side of the road. Neither could identify it as anything they had ever heard of or seen.

Years later, Roger decided to tell this story to an Arizona State Trooper that he met. The trooper not only seemed unsurprised but said that another trooper he knew refused to patrol that highway after dark, due to a local legend about a "coyote man." The trooper advised Roger not to travel that road after sunset, either.

Chapter 9

Kansas: More Than Dust in the Wind

Kansas Silo Kreeper

Kansas is not known for the type of watery, forested areas that host large, furred cryptids in other states. But this Great Plains state does have one important creature-friendly feature: endless fields that provide cover and attract prey species like deer, raccoons, and even birds. Besides, one thing I have learned is that manwolves do not require deep wilderness thickets, and are often attracted to certain areas such as roads and cemeteries that are frequented by humans.

Kansas is the source of a weird and scary report associated with another recurring cryptid theme—military bases. It came from a man named Jeff, who wrote me in May, 2006, about his experience in 1973 when he was only thirteen. He lived south of Wichita at the time, near an old Boeing military property that he would often explore stealthily at night with friends.

The property's main attraction was an abandoned military silo. The boys had to squirm twelve feet up the riveted seams to reach the lower rungs of the service ladders that still hung from the top. Their next daring act was to crawl across the silo's domed top to the interior ladder that they could use to reach the inside bottom, which was home to hundreds of pigeons. The boys then caught birds to take home and train as homing pigeons. Since the area was not lit, they only went to the silo on nights of the full moon.

One night, Jeff said, the area around the silo was entirely silent; no crickets or other nighttime noises broke the stillness. They continued anyway, but stopped about one hundred yards from the silo, as they noticed a "figure" atop the very challenging structure.

At first they thought they had a human competitor for their pigeon scheme and decided to skulk through some bushes for a better look. But as they approached the silo, they realized it was a large dog.

"We whispered to each other about how this could be," he wrote, "and the creature heard us. The creature then stood up on two hind feet and was clearly silhouetted in the moonlight. The head was very canine, mouth open with a large ruff around the neck. The body was canine but also human."

The muzzle was larger than a German shepherd's, he added, and the creature's very large teeth were plainly visible.

"We should have run at that point," Jeff continued, "but being thirteen we egged each other on and got false courage by pretending to be brave. I myself was terrified. We walked in a large perimeter of the silo with the beast turning and following our every move, the whole time snarling a chilling low growl. We could not get closer. The silo was about forty feet tall and maybe twenty feet wide and if you got closer he'd slip out of view due to the silo blocking our line of sight. We really didn't want to get closer because we could tell that whatever this was, it was very dangerous."

Finally, the creature let out a raspy, "mixed bark-howl sound," and the boys ran. They told no one about the creature but decided to go back in daylight a few days later. They managed to thread their way through the woods and brush only to climb the silo and find the hatch closed on top.

"This was something we never did," he said, "as it would trap the birds, and they would die a terrible death of thirst in the dark."

They did finally pull the hatch open and train their flashlights inside. Normally the silo was alive with roosting birds, but the boys could not see or hear them, so they climbed down for a better look. Little did they dream of the horror that awaited them at the bottom.

"There was nothing alive," said Jeff. "It was as if something had put a blender in the silo and turned it on; there were bird parts and bird blood everywhere on the walls and across the floor. We left and never went back."

The silo has since been removed, he said, but the memory of the creature remains. "We know it had a canine face and neck, we knew it growled, and was somehow capable of getting on top of a forty-foot metal silo, killing everything in it and scaring the hell out of us."

Jeff had become a forty-five-year-old business owner by the time he wrote to me, but he added that he always felt there was an element of the paranormal in the experience, due to the complete silence of the natural world in the creature's presence. This is a feature that I've heard in many other reports, such as that of John Lyons in Michigan. I am not sure whether it implies super-awareness on the part of wildlife (why would crickets be that afraid of a single carnivore?) or if it indicates an electromagnetic or time/space anomaly that may be occurring, according to researchers like Paul Devereaux in *The Haunted Land*, when archetypal images such as wolfmen are encountered. The one thing experiencers of "the silence" agree upon is that it is ultra-creepy.

Chapter 10

Minnesota Monsters

Leaving the sunny Southwest for the frigid climes of Minnesota, which of course lies just to the west of the Mississippi, it becomes apparent that either the dogman knows how to swim or he has learned to sneak across bridges. There are not as many reports from Minnesota as I would expect, given the state's nearness to Werewolf Central (southern Wisconsin), but I have received more and more as public awareness of the phenomena has grown. I guess that if Brett Favre could find his way westward from Packers tundra to Vikings turf, an intelligent manwolf could, too.

Vastly predating (and likely outlasting) Favre in Minnesota, the creature may have been there for at least 60 years or more. I have found vague references to a bipedal, dogman-like creature sighted just north of Minneapolis in Coon Rapids in the 1950s, as well as a stronger report of a creature that frightened a young southern Minnesota man a decade later. Brad Steiger, famed author of *The Werewolf Book: An Encyclopedia of Shape-Shifting Beings*, shared a report with me he received from one of his students when he was an English and literature professor at Luther College in Decorah, Iowa, in the 1960s. Steiger called the incident "one of the best reports I have ever heard," and I agree with that assessment, particularly since dogmen were not at all in the public consciousness at that time.

Big Butt Beastie

Steiger described the student as a "well-mannered" young man, a biology/pre-med student enrolled in one of Steiger's core classes for freshmen in 1963. The student finished the course, and Steiger did not see him again until 1967, after the young man had started dating a student secretary in the college's English department. She brought him to Steiger, who by then was becoming known for writing books about the strange and paranormal, and insisted he tell his former professor about a bizarre experience he'd had the previous weekend.

The student had been driving from his home back to Luther College after dark when he saw what he thought was a very large wolf feeding on some kind of animal carcass on the shoulder of the road. Curious, the student slowed his car to illuminate the creature in his headlights and then parked just in front of it for a better look.

That turned out to be impossible. To his shock, the animal stood up on its hind legs to reach a height of about six feet and let forth a menacing growl. Before the student could react, it turned and made for a stand of trees. The student had a very good look at its backside and realized with surprise that it showed a "pronounced buttocks." That would not be surprising if the animal were a baboon, but prominent rear ends are not a trait of canines or most other quadrupeds.

Since the creature with the badonkadonk butt had apparently fled, the student grabbed a flashlight to see what it had been eating for dinner before he interrupted it. The meal turned out to be a rabbit, which the creature evidently wanted back. It had by then reached the vantage point of a small hill, from which it stood and roared. The student decided that discretion truly is the better part of valor, hopped back in his vehicle, and told no one but his girlfriend.

Steiger remembers him as a non-drinking, unimaginative rationalist, not the type to make something like this up. I do have to say that, except for the strange derriere, this was a classic manwolf-type sighting, right down to the height, description as wolf-like, the road-kill supper and the action of rising up when surprised. And this occurred twenty years before the first publicity of the Michigan Dogman and thirty-five years before the first Beast of Bray Road article. And it is not the last Minnesota sighting I know of.

Beast of Biwabik

The Iron Range of Minnesota lies along a line of ore formations in the state's northern section, bounded by vast tracts of lake-drenched national forests, within easy prowling range of Lake Superior. If there was ever an area that might attract reclusive mammalian predators—or ancient nature spirits seeking deep wilderness—this would be it.

One man who grew up on seven wooded acres near Biwabik, a bit east of Hibbing, can vouch for that assumption. Adam wrote after seeing the July, 2009, *Sean Hannity Show* when my dogman sketches reminded him of something he glimpsed on his family's land around 1991, at the age of twelve.

"One afternoon in the summer," he wrote, "I was walking around the woods near my house with a BB gun, pretending I was a hunter. I heard what sounded like a very loud sneeze fairly far off in the woods. The sound repeated itself and started getting louder.

"After a few seconds, some motion caught my eye, and about one hundred yards from where I was standing, a large dark creature was bounding through the woods on its hind legs at an extremely fast pace. I got really scared and crouched next to a brush pile as it ran. The animal was at least seven feet tall in my opinion."

Adam was relieved when his dog suddenly came running past him and tore through the woods, barking loudly at the creature. The dog returned safely, and Adam ran to fetch his father and brother from their house. They searched for prints or other evidence but found nothing, so they did not report the event to authorities.

"Needless to say," he added, "the moment I saw the images of werewolves on *Hannity*, this came to mind. Not sure what it was, but similarly, this took place in the northern woods."

From Adam's description, I think it is safe to say this was not a bear running fast on its hind legs.

It could possibly have been a Bigfoot, but it was the dogman image that clicked with him in an era when everyone is very familiar with what Sasquatch and kin are supposed to look like.

The Pickwick Manpup

In November, 2007, a Luther College student named Amanda wrote to tell me she had been criticized her whole life for believing in werewolves, but that her belief stemmed from an incident that happened when she was in middle school, in the late 1990s.

She grew up in the Mississippi River town of Winona in southeastern Minnesota, just twenty miles or so north of La Crosse, Wisconsin, where I investigated a fall, 2006 sighting of a man-sized furry creature with bat-like, ten-foot wings that attacked two men in a pickup truck (detailed in *Strange Wisconsin: More Badger State Weirdness*). It is also just across the river from Trempealeau, home to a sacred hill and the remains of an ancient Mississippian pyramid complex (again see *Strange Wisconsin*).

She wrote:

"A friend named Elizabeth and I were on our way back from a dance called 'fun night' to her father's home in Pickwick, Minnesota. Her father owns a cabin-like home on the edge of a somewhat desolate stretch of forest. As we were riding up the hill with Elizabeth's father driving, Liz and I passed the time chatting about the dance when her father stopped the car abruptly and shined the light out across the field.

"What we saw really messed with my perception of reality. It wasn't the typical Hollywood perception of a werewolf, but if I had to take a stab, I'd relate it to that creature. It stood on two legs and was about five feet tall. It had the face of a coyote or wolf, that distinct, pointy snout, and a darker coat of fur. It had a long tail, unlike a black bear, and it was thinner as opposed to the extra chub you see on bears."

As so often happens in such encounters, the humans and the creature stared at one another for what was probably a few seconds, and then it walked off into the woods on its hind legs, showing no fear or hurry.

"When you see something like that," said Amanda, "there aren't many options when you don't have a photo or any kind of evidence but your true and sincere word to back you up. I have two other witnesses as well, Liz and her father, and we were all equally shaken by this incident, still feeling the effects after all these years."

Yes, Amanda, that lack of other evidence is always the unfortunate problem. Amanda's story with all its details and the other two witnesses rings very true for me, however, and I feel it is a credible account.

Creature of Crosslake

The man who wrote about the next encounter asked several times that I withhold his identity, and since his real first name is unique, I will just call him Bob.

Bob's brush with beastliness came in the summer of 2007 as he drove north from Minneapolis to his relative's home in Crosslake. He was about a mile south of the town, which would have closely sandwiched him between Whitefish Lake and Crow Wing State Forest, with the Cuyuna Iron Range lying just to the east. It was not yet dusk, so his visibility was excellent.

As he drove that final mile, he saw something that astounded him.

"Up ahead on the east side of the highway in the ditch, well outside the tree line, was the biggest wolf I had ever seen. I mean this was big. It was on all fours but had its back hunched up like a cat's when they are trying to ward something off. I slowed down rapidly and pulled over, thinking it was going to run off into the woods, but it didn't. It just stood there staring at me from about twenty-five to thirty feet away."

At that point, Bob could feel his heart begin to race. "There was something very wrong with this picture. It was not just a giant wolf. It was built differently. There was something different about the arms and legs from how a wolf's or dog's legs are connected or shaped. It had almost human qualities to it."

Bob estimated that he stared at the creature for at least a minute and a half (although witnesses frequently overestimate the actual length of such incidents) and watched the creature return his stare, immobile, its lips curled back in a frozen snarl.

"The bizarre thing was that looking in its eyes, there was high intelligence there. I mean, you look in a dog's eyes or another animal's and there is no sense of 'knowing.' The feeling that I had at this time was that this thing was highly intelligent and calculating me. I knew I was in danger. I was very ready to punch the gas and almost did when it dropped its back down low and took a few steps slowly toward me in stalking fashion.

"As I took my foot off the brake to punch the gas, I hit the horn. The strange thing that has kept me from talking about it is that it turned around to run into the woods but *stood up and took five steps on its hind legs before dropping back down to all fours and running off into the woods*!" (Emphasis mine)

Bob sat there, stunned, but the creature did not return, so he finally continued to his relative's house, and the relative told him she had seen TV shows about dogmen. He said that up until then, he had been too skeptical to watch that kind of show and would roll his eyes when others talked about such things.

"But I know what I saw," he said—a refrain I hear from many adamant witnesses—"and although a minute and a half is not that long a time, it was plenty for me to examine this freak of nature. It was very close so I could see it was a live animal. Now I don't go into the woods anymore, fishing or camping, without carrying my Glock 10mm pistol. Had I been walking, I know this thing would have attacked."

I would like to note that Bob's keen awareness of the creature's sentience is something I also hear very frequently from witnesses that make close eye contact with manwolves. They feel the creature is somehow more than a mere animal. Some have suggested that this trait, along with Bob's observation of joints and limbs that appeared somewhat human, might put this particular creature in the Skinwalker, or magically conjured being, category. Bob, however, felt sure he had seen a live—if unidentifiable—animal, and that judgment came as the result of a long and close look in daylight conditions. I think Bob is probably smart to carry his Glock in those dark Minnesota woods.

PART THREE

East of the Mississippi

Chapter 11

Illinois: Land of Lincoln Dogs

The landscape of Illinois is similar to that of Kansas with its flat plains and massive tracts of cropland. Its Lake Michigan shores have been swallowed by the urban juggernaut of Chicago and environs. It does not, therefore, sound like a promising place to find cryptids, but apparently the creatures don't know that. Neither do the witnesses. In my previous books I've documented the giant, car-attacking black panther of Wadsworth, the Anubis-like dogman at the Great Lakes Naval Base north of Chicago, four bipedal canine window peepers in Decatur, and a cluster of dogman sightings around Freeport that occurred during 2002-2003.

Orchard Anomaly

Those sightings inspired other Illinois witnesses to write, and one man named Mike sent a doozy from the village of Hardin, about forty miles north of St. Louis, Missouri, from around 1970. Although he was only ten years old that year, Mike had no trouble recalling the events of the summer evening when he wandered outside to play in an orchard just across the road from his house.

"I hadn't walked but a few yards when I thought I'd heard something behind me a little ways," he wrote. "I turned, but couldn't see anything in the dark, and I had no flashlight. After standing there for a minute or two, I turned and started walking again, only to hear a rustling sound like leaves were being brushed against. I again stopped and turned, but could neither see nor hear anything."

As soon as Mike started to walk again, the leaf-crunching also resumed behind him, and he realized he was being followed. He started running back to his house, a distance he estimated at about the length of a football field, and finally reached his front porch, gasping for breath. One of the family's dogs lit out past him in the direction of the road and orchard, but it returned quickly with tail between its legs and ran under the safe haven of the porch.

Mike then looked back at the orchard and saw what had been stalking him, as the dogs barked their muzzles off at it.

"It looked like a German shepherd or a wolf walking on its hind legs," he wrote, "appearing to be seven to eight feet tall. Its fur was dark, even where the lights from the front porch and the driveway were shining on it. It stood there for a few seconds, probably no more than a minute, looking around. It only glanced briefly at me or the dogs, seeming to ignore all of us, then turned and ran down the road to the southwest away from the house. That's when I ran into the house and told my family what had happened. They all came outside, but saw nothing as the creature was long gone. They laughed and told me I watched too many monster movies before going back into the house."

The next day, Mike felt bold enough to go back to the orchard in the bright daylight. He searched a wide area of the orchard and surrounding woods for prints but found nothing. He remembers that at the same time there were reports of Bigfoot sightings around Louisiana and Missouri, but said, "I certainly didn't see anything resembling a Bigfoot." What he saw, he said, "remarkably resembled" my dogman drawing on *Monsterquest's* "American Werewolf" episode.

Dog Eat Dog

The small town of Millstadt lies just southeast of St. Louis, Missouri, not much more than ten miles from the Mississippi River, and dates back to a cluster of German immigrants who plunked themselves down there in 1836. A surprising number of village residents are descendants of those first settlers, and they have preserved many of the town's charming, original brick buildings. Perhaps they have preserved something else, too.

Sturdy settlers and old architecture notwithstanding, Millstadt's history is a bit on the macabre side. In 1874, the town became nationally infamous for the gruesome ax murders of five members of the Carl

Steltezenreide family. The land where the family farmstead once stood is said to have been haunted ever since and indeed would appear to be a classic, John Keel-style "window area" where all manner of unexplainable things are prone to leach into our workaday world.

In the 1980s, area residents reported seeing Bigfoot and black panthers lurking about.

Then there are the UFOs. On July 4, 1997, Millstadt was one of a string of southern Illinois towns to see one or more blue-green objects zip through the night sky. Hundreds of people witnessed the enigmatic sky craft, with sightings at several different times over Millstadt. And in January, 2000, Millstadt police officer Craig Stevens was one of those to witness a triangular, lighted object tracking slowly above the town as it emitted a low-decibel hum.

In December, 2007, a Millstadt resident named Jim Bostick wrote to tell me that a rural byway outside of town, Zing Road, known locally as a haunted lane, was the site of an unknown creature incident in the late 1990s. A female friend was chased in her car by a huge, fur-covered quadruped with a wolf-like head.

Another friend, however, had a much scarier encounter in the same time frame about two miles away off Concordia Church Road. (Bostick provided both friends' full names, to be withheld). This friend was a male in his mid-teens at the time, and one night had to go outside in search of his eighty-pound, white German shepherd which had uncharacteristically escaped from the house and set off for the woods.

Picking his way through the dark woods with his flashlight, he had gone about one quarter mile when he heard growling ahead. He followed it to a clearing of high weeds lit by the moon and could hear his dog barking. Figuring the dog was tussling with a raccoon or a coyote, he called the dog's name but heard only more sounds of animals struggling in the shaking weeds.

It wasn't his dog that he saw first, however. It was a seven-to-eight foot, muscular creature with a man-like body covered in shaggy fur and a head like that of a wolf. It stood on its hind legs and to the teen's utter horror, then picked up the German shepherd with its paws and tore it in two. The teen did not wait to see what happened next but ran stumbling back to his house, trying not to hear the awful noises still coming from the clearing.

The next day he went back to the woods and found only blood, fur and other remains. His family believed the dog was killed by coyotes. Ten years after the incident, said Bostick, his friend was still shaken over his pet's bizarre demise.

Cryptozoo of Zion

Many Illinois sightings occur in the northern part of the state, especially near the Wisconsin border. Zion, a city originally founded as a religious Utopia, lies just south of that border in the extreme northeast corner of Illinois. I have written about it in my book, *The Poison Widow*. It was the final refuge of convicted 1920s poison murderer Myrtle Schaude, and her second family there never knew who she really was until I told them.

A more recent resident named Allen wrote me in August, 2009, to share what happened to him there in May, 1987. He had just recently moved there from the city that year and was having trouble adjusting to the quiet nights. One evening he decided to take a relaxing walk in the hope that it would make him sleepy.

He ended up walking south on Hwy 173, which at that time followed a route down to Lake Michigan. He came to a guard rail and ditch in front of some old railroad tracks, stopped to light a cigarette and then continued past the remains of an abandoned subdivision before finishing his mile-long trek to the lakeshore. He smoked a few more cigarettes, tossed a few driftwood chunks into the water, and then headed back up the path to the road.

Halfway there, he had to pass through a knot of trees that darkened the path. He was a little nervous about going through the dark spot, he said, and that fear was justified when at about 500 feet from the trees he saw a dark figure standing in the path ahead. He assumed it was just another late night walker, until the figure turned to reveal its profile.

"It was distinctly broad across the shoulders," Allen said, "and much more slender in the midsection. It had an extended, canine-like muzzle and LONG arms that must have been down past its knees. I stopped and stared intently trying to focus on what I was seeing. It took one step and was off the road on my left side.

"To say I was a little bothered by this would be a huge understatement. It was no more than ten to fifteen seconds later that I heard something running and splashing and tearing through the brush and marsh on my left moving fast. I turned and followed the noise and looked back the way I had just came, and out from the side the thing stepped and again stopped in the center of the road and just stood there."

Allen felt desperate to get out of the area and worse, knew he still had to go through that dark patch of trees. At this time he could hear the creature running through the brush to his right. He walked faster. He had almost made it through the dark place when the creature stepped into his path again but at a much closer distance. He stopped, feeling the animal was toying with him.

Taking a better look this time, he estimated its height at between seven and eight feet tall standing on its hind legs in a "stooped" posture. It had ears "pinned back" on top of its head (canines flatten their ears as a warning). It stepped off the road again and disappeared again, but Allen listened warily as it followed him to the railroad tracks. After Allen had crossed the tracks, he turned to look behind him one last time and saw the creature standing there, still watching him.

"I really did feel like I was being toyed with," he finished, "this thing knew that at any time it could have ended me, and I think it wanted me to know it as well."

Just to put the location in context, the Zion shore lies between two other Lake Michigan sightings: the one mentioned earlier at Great Lakes Naval Base and a 2007 sighting in South Milwaukee you will read about in Part Four, the section on newer Wisconsin reports.

And although Allen did not say whether he continued his midnight lake strolls, I think it is safe to assume he found another way to go to sleep after that.

Algonquin Animal

Sean from Algonquin, four miles south of Crystal Lake, wrote that he has never been much for ghosts and goblins. But while driving home one night around 2002 from a dance club in Elgin, about ten miles south of Algonquin, he saw something that he says still chills and confuses him.

Sean was the designated driver for his small group of friends that night and had not been drinking. It was three or four in the morning on a snowy winter night, and Sean said he was focused on keeping his car on the road as he drove north on State Hwy 31. His friends were awake and chatting as the car wound through slippery roads that curved around farms and woodlands.

"The stretch of 31 we were on was a two-lane road, with a steep hill on the left, thick woods and a downward slope to the right that was also thick woods," Sean wrote.

"About a hundred or so feet ahead of me, I will never forget, a shape leaped across the road in about two bounds. It leaped from the right side of the road across to the left side and up into the woods there, then vanished. I was sober, and I was wide awake.

"The creature was large and I would say a grayish color, but that could be because of all the snow. I would definitely say for sure that it moved too fast to be a bear, and it was too large to be a deer or an actual dog, but leaped fast and had back leg motion like a deer would. It had a lot of fur, like a wolf. With the way it moved...I would have to say it was some kind of werewolf-like creature, and no, not like in any werewolf movie I have ever seen."

Sean said that after this incident he carried a sword in his car for months and is still paranoid about driving at night. He now carries a camera, hoping to be ready to capture anything else he might see on film.

Warlock Hermit Werewolf

As any reader will have deduced by now, there is an ongoing debate whether cryptids like dogmen are "real"—but unknown—animals, transient visitors from elsewhere, or just a little something whipped up by your local magic practitioner. Illinois researcher Derek Grebner passed along a story from his own family that supports the latter belief. His Slavic great-grandfather, Jack Ratliff, told him a tale that dates back to the 1930s in the north central part of the state, just north of Peoria, outside Chillicothe.

Chillicothe, wouldn't you know it, lies along the Illinois River, with state parks and forests to the west and east. Jack Ratliff's land lay in a valley bounded by the Santa Fe Railroad tracks, and he believed it was once a Native American burial ground. Ratliff farmed and trapped the land, so he knew it well. Here is Derek's great-grandfather's story, in Derek's own words.

"He also told me of great boars and wolves that once roamed the land, and of the Indian burial ground within the valley of his home. But one story he told me I never took much to until I saw a sketch by Linda S. Godfrey, and began reading her work, *Hunting the American Werewolf*, that chronicles lycanthrope sightings in the United States. When I saw her 'beast kneeling with road-kill sketch,' this old story was brought to mind.

"Jack started to notice that during the trapping season, on the nights and times of the full moon his traps would be raided. Whatever had been in them was gone, the de-gloved part of the foot left behind and some bloody and large tracks. The tracks looked very suspicious because they looked like whatever made them walked on two legs; there was no front paw track. When his trapping season would end on the full moon a chicken would go missing and its blood would be on the floor of the hen house.

"The hen house had a plank floor and was made from good wood, and has a latch on the door. Jack was tired of losing money so one night my great granddad took out his lantern and single shot twelve gauge with rock salt shells and a corn knife. He could hear something in the hen house so he very quietly opened the latched door and went in, setting the lantern on its peg. He immediately threw the butt of the shotgun to his shoulder as the light illuminated a hunched over creature.

"With a snout and pointed ears, it was holding a chicken with upturned palms like a man would. It was very hairy and appeared to be kneeling. The creature had the head of a wolf and arms like a man's with claw fingers. It almost had a mane. The creature looked up and dropped the chicken when it noticed Granddad. It stood up on two legs like a man and howled, taking a few menacing steps at Jack, who cocked the shotgun and at a range of about ten feet discharged the load of rock salt into the creature. It was knocked almost to the ground and was howling in pain, but it came closer and Jack swung his shotgun by the barrel and busted the stock right off the gun on the creature. The creature, in pain and now possibly in fear, ran to the back of the hen house breaking out the back planks with its speed, and it was lost to the night.

"The terror was never seen again and most likely left the district. Other men shared stories about having piglets snatched and traps raided. Later in the year Jack found cached bones from small animals and large animals that had been gnawed by large teeth. However, the old hen house had been bulldozed, and all the bones lost.

"There was an overpass for the railroad that created a bridge over a road, and under this bridge had lived a pagan hermit. His disappearance from the valley for parts unknown coincided with the end of the hen house raids. The hermit was known to use magic rituals. The sub-story voiced to me by my great-granddad was that the hermit was some kind of warlock who made a deal with the devil and became an agent of darkness. My great-granddad is dead and has been for years and so are all those who lived and would be able to take a (polygraph) test.

"He showed me once a set of silver bullets he had made after his ordeal. Being a Slav he knew what he had seen. However, after his death (a relative) pilfered the house and anything of value was stripped from it."

As a correspondent for the Center for Fortean Zoology (cfz.org.uk), Grebner has also documented numerous sightings of bears, cougars, wolves and even Bigfoot in Illinois. But this sighting sounds like none of those. It would indeed have been nice if Jack Ratliff had been able to preserve the gnawed bones or silver bullets. But it should be noted that in the Great Depression era of the 1930s, many communities had their share of homeless men, who sometimes ended up living as hermits. They were often viewed with suspicion by townspeople, and it doesn't surprise me that one would come to be known as a warlock. And a secretive, stealthy man could have been stealing chickens and piglets without the aid of any magic werewolfery.

Still, that does not explain what Jack Ratliff saw in the henhouse, and the story is very reminiscent of other reports involving farm buildings and small livestock. Add one more to the mystery pile.

Central Strangeness

A little farther south of Jack Ratliff's farm, from around Springfield in Sangamon, Morgan and Macoupin Counties, Jacksonville researcher Larry J. White of a group called SCIPP—Society of Christians Investigating Paranormal Phenomena—sent me a slew of summarized reports. Regrettably, dates are not included and I was not able to learn any more about the second-hand stories, but the fact that other groups are also hearing about wolf-like cryptids helps bolster the possibility that something weird and canine may really be there.

In Sangamon County, White noted his group had received several reports of furred, wolf-like creatures. Two of the reports were from Chatham. The first one said a wolf-like creature was sighted around

midnight peeping into a window (another familiar action). It then rummaged through some trash cans before leaping a four-foot fence and running away. The second report came from a group of teens walking outside Chatham in a cornfield during the wee morning hours, when they encountered a "slim looking, brown haired dog-beast with red eyes."

Macoupin County apparently hosts the Dogman Senior Citizen Den, as several people have reported a bald, red-eyed man-like creature that seems to be searching for something.

White says that Morgan County, where SCIPP's headquarters is located, is "probably the most active sightings county in Illinois." He lists the following events:

"In Lake Jacksonville, several people witnessed a glowing red-eyed beast drinking from the lake on many separate occasions at night time. I asked these people what it looked like with more detail, they replied, 'It looked like a dog/human mix except it was the size of an eight-year-old child, with pulsating glowing red eyes.' I then asked these people if they might have thought it was a prank. They replied, 'Heavens no.'

"One guy shot a flare gun close by the creature and said it just stood still, like it wasn't scared. I sent my 'creature' investigator Chris to investigate the local timber surrounding the spot the creature was sighted, but the only thing found was a baby rattle and a raccoon carcass. I had Chris take a team of five to comb a two-mile radius around the lake, but still nothing was found.

"At S.C.I.P.P. Headquarters, I had turned onto our side street, just about to turn into our drive when I noticed a single glowing, red, quarter-sized, round object across the street near an old garage. I quickly ran in and got my flashlight and ran outside, it was still there. My light is a spot light, so I shined it in the direction of the red spot and it disappeared. Thinking it was a kid playing with a laser pointer, I started to turn around when I heard a hideous screech that lasted for a minute. I walked over to where I heard this sound and shined my light; there was a black mass with one red eye. It ran across the neighbor's backyard, so I chased after it, but lost it a block away. I never seen it again, but won't forget its screeching sound and the horrible smell that filled the back yard."

Offered merely as supporting evidence of a tradition of werewolf lore in this state, I also found a folk tale of a red-eyed canine in Illinois in the southern third of the state, east of St. Louis in Washington County. Author Tom Hollatz includes it in his *Campfire Collection: Haunts, Taunts and Unexplained Tales* published by Angel Press, 1993. It's a traditional witch tale involving a farmer harassed by a huge, red-eyed wolf that returned night after night to tear the throats out of his pigs. The farmer was finally able to get rid of the beast by shooting it in its left front leg, and he was surprised to later encounter an elderly neighbor suspected of witchery with a gunshot wound to the corresponding place in her left arm.

The author gave no date for the story, but evidently it occurred before wolves became a protected species. And for the record, I don't recommend shooting suspected werewolves. You never know for sure just what—or who—they may be.

Motorola Stalker

I am always grateful to folks who take the time to write out their experiences in great detail even when events don't quite fit the manwolf mold. I will tuck a couple of these in here for what they are worth, before moving on to richer fare. They are interesting stories even if they do lend only indirect support.

A man who needs to remain anonymous for reasons that will be obvious wrote in May, 2007, to tell of something that frightened him when he used to work in the now closed, gigantic Motorola plant in Harvard, near the border with Walworth County, Wisconsin.

From spring through fall of 2002, he found himself homeless, so he secretly slept on a camping mattress in his office, using the restrooms and office kitchen when the rest of the staff had gone home. Twice he was discovered by maintenance crew who kept his secret. The plant was already in its final years and was running on a skeleton staff, so it was easier for him to get away with living in his second floor area with electronic entry. He even had a nice view of an adjacent pond where deer came to drink. He did not use alcohol or drugs.

One night, he was awakened by an incredibly powerful, musky, skunk-like odor which seemed to be coming from right outside his office door. He froze and held his breath, but heard nothing. After a while the smell diminished. He did find a garbage can knocked over the next day, just outside, but no evidence of what could have made the odor. I can only imagine a spectral Bigfoot or manwolf.

Another morning, very early on a Saturday, he awoke to hear strange, animal-like screams that he could not identify. Something carnivorous hunting at the pond, perhaps? I don't blame him for not opening his door to look, but I can't help wishing he had.

I should mention that Harvard is only about a twenty-minute drive from several Wisconsin sightings detailed in *Hunting*, including the 2004 report on Stateline Road near Sharon and the 2005 report on White Pigeon Road of what sounded like a young Bigfoot. And it is just east of a whole cluster of disturbing sightings in eastern Winnebago County.

Winnebago County Wild Things

Very few dogman witnesses have the chance to see the creature twice, but sometimes it happens, and seldom by choice. One woman who lives in a rural location only a few miles south of the Wisconsin border was one of the "lucky" ones. She had no fewer than three sightings between December and June, 2006, in her own backyard. These reports were sent to me by a very careful investigator, S.J. Saladino, who promised the witnesses he would keep their identities and location secret.

The first incident happened one night while the middle-aged woman was babysitting her granddaughter. They heard what sounded like one of their cats suddenly yowling from the backyard and rushed to the kitchen patio door. The wooded yard is lit by a mercury vapor light, and they could see a tall figure standing on two feet about fifteen feet from the house. The woman banged on the glass door, hoping to startle whoever seemed to be hurting her cat.

That is when the dark figure turned to look at them, and they could see it was not a "whoever" but a "whatever." To their shock, it had the head of a wolf and was covered in very dark fur. They estimated it stood six feet tall. And their cat was clamped in its jaws.

Luckily for the cat, the creature was indeed so startled at seeing the women that it dropped the cat and ran on all fours into the shadows. I assume the cat gave up only one of its nine lives that night.

The next incident occurred in March, while the woman's thirty-year-old son was there. She was outside in the yard when the creature emerged on all fours from the back of the property. She called her son, who came quickly and was armed. Strangely, the animal stood staring at them while turning its head side to side as it made a strange sound the woman described as an "ooooh." (I have never heard that behavior before.) The son tried to creep closer for a better look, but the creature turned and ran.

She was alone for the last encounter. Her house has a "cat door" near the floor in one room, and one day in June she was surprised to see not a cat but the head of something that looked like a mini-version of the backyard creature trying to enter. She speculated that this was one of the big thing's pups. She and other family members also heard canine vocalizations of varying pitches during and following these months. And this was not the family's last incident.

In July, the woman's husband finally faced their backyard visitor. The couple had been awakened at two in the morning by canine growls and by the screeching of one or more frightened cats. The husband stepped cautiously into the front yard and saw the strange canine pad out on all fours from behind a truck in the driveway, then run away when it saw the husband. He reported that the beast had to measure at least thirty-four inches tall at the shoulder, since it stood much higher than the rear bumper of the half ton pickup.

Saladino said he planned to continue to monitor the situation, and he did include a few more salient details that the homeowners requested not be made public. I sincerely hope the creature or creatures found the yard too well populated by pesky humans to allow easy cat-hunting, and that they took off for wilder pastures.

Freeport Road-Bounder

Heading straight west from Harvard and through Rockford, we arrive at the 2002-2003 cluster of sightings around Freeport. But someone else had an encounter in that same area only a couple of years earlier. A woman unrelated to the 2002-2003 events wrote:

"I am writing at the encouragement of my husband, who is very into cryptozoology and is reading *Hunting the American Werewolf* right now. A little about me—I am 41, married for seventeen years, the parent of one child and a native of the Chicago area. I currently live in Freeport, IL and work in the social services. I consider myself to be level-headed and grounded in reality. Weird things do not generally happen to me! But several years ago I saw something really strange.

"In the winter of either 1999 or 2000, I was driving alone from Freeport to Springfield, IL for a meeting of a professional organization I belonged to at the time. I was traveling south on I-39 and was somewhere between LaSalle-Peru and Bloomington, IL. It was early afternoon on an overcast day. The ground was snow-covered, traffic was light.

"I caught a movement in my peripheral vision on the left and saw something on the divide that my mind registered as a huge wolf, which immediately leapt over the road on which I was traveling (both lanes) in front of me in one bound. I was driving rather fast and am not an overly confident driver so I gripped the wheel (shaken by the near miss) and did not turn to see where the animal had headed.

"I remember clearly even now some unusual features of this 'wolf'—it was huge! I am not great at estimating the size of things, but in full run/jump it nearly spanned both lanes of the road from outstretched front legs to outstretched back legs; it was running on all fours but its limbs were extremely long and its movements were graceful. Its head was small in relation to its body; its snout/muzzle was thin but very pronounced; its ears were small but pointy and stood straight up; its fur was an unusual gray-black (neither gray nor black—never saw anything like it).

"I have reflected many times on the sighting and often wonder what in the world this was! I did some research about wolf sightings in central Illinois (and read that black wolves have been sighted in the Peoria area, which is not terribly far from where I was). But I honestly think this was something else."

Although this particular creature was not observed on its hind legs, there are several factors that warrant its inclusion as a report. The credibility of the witness as a middle-aged social worker on her way to a professional meeting in broad daylight makes it hard to cast aspersions on her motivations, state of mind or ability to observe the creature.

Its unusual appearance and behavior, though, are what put it in the suspicious canine category. As I have noted often, these creatures seem to be adept at getting around on either four or two legs, and staying on all fours would make a reclusive beast much less noticeable. The woman may well have had a brush with an Illinois Dogman in quadrupedal mode.

Strangely, there is a long-standing tradition of another creature that does walk upright not far from Peoria: the Kewanee Deerman. In May, 2007, journalist Dave Clarke of the *Kewanee Star Courier* wrote several columns about the creature, which began skulking around Kewanee in the 1950s and early 60s, mostly near Johnson Sauk Trail State Park. Deerman walked bipedally like a human but had the body, head and antlers of a deer. Word was that to see the Deerman three times was lethal.

Deerman pawed at the car windows of parking couples, was spotted hiding in at least one outhouse and had one glowing, red eye. According to Clarke, most locals believe Deerman is a mere campfire tale that may have been inspired by a taxidermist with a spare trophy buck head and a little too much time on his hooves.

Just for the record, a few witnesses have described the body of upright manwolves as reminding them of a deer standing up. And there once lived a horrific wolf-like mammal called *Andrewsarchus* which would have stood six feet tall at the shoulder and had multiple hooves for toes. But that was 40 million years ago.

Author's sketch of *Andrewsarchus*

Chapter 12

From Indiana Impossibles to Ohio Oddness

Only one thing stands between Illinois and Ohio, and that is Indiana, a state bounded to the south by the Ohio River and to the north by a chunk of Lake Michigan shore. A combination of open plains, rolling uplands and lowland forests, parts of the state are rich in valleys, ridges and cavern systems, including the massive Wyandotte Cave, third largest in the U.S. with twenty-three miles of passageways. It lies only twenty-five miles from the Kentucky border. I've always thought that natural caverns would provide logical hideouts for canids that wanted to avoid the spotlight, and southern Indiana has them in spades.

Fairmount Biped

It was almost forty years ago, in 1971, that a young woman from Fairmount, Indiana, saw what she thought was a cow. Fairmount is seventy miles northeast of Indianapolis, less than ten miles from the Mississinewa River and about fifty miles from Ohio—due west of a line of sightings in that state.

She was driving on a rural road in early fall, and it was a warm evening so her windows were down and radio on. She was only doing about forty miles per hour, so she had plenty of time to observe the huge animal leap a fence to her left—and land upright on two legs!

At that point, she had a hunch this was no cow. And it was close.

"It gracefully stepped on the road beside the front of the car," she said, "As my car passed it (I could have put my hand out of the window and touched it, it was that close), it put its left 'arm' and 'hand' on the roof of the car and down and across the trunk of the car…as it crossed the road behind me.

"It happened so fast. As close as it was—although I did look in the rearview mirror as it went behind the car—I couldn't see anything but a dark form. It was large, definitely not a man, maybe larger than a man. Fright may have made it seem more large. But cars in the 70s were bigger than now, and it lifted its arm to drag it across the roof of my car."

When Betty checked her car for damage the next morning, she saw drag marks where the creature's limb had brushed through the dust her car had accumulated from her frequent drives on dirt roads. The marks trailed over the roof and then across the trunk, just as she had observed.

She was sure this was not a Sasquatch. "I've heard about Bigfoot," she said. "This wasn't Bigfoot. Maybe, just maybe, almost forty years ago I saw one of your creatures."

I think that this witness did a good job of analyzing her perceptions—wondering if she exaggerated its size, for instance. But there is no getting around the fact that the creature she saw not only jumped and landed on two feet, but it had to remain bipedal in order for its arm to swipe the top of her car. As usual, I pine for photos never taken of the evidence; in this case I would have been keen to have seen a picture of the dust disturbance.

Hardin Ridge Creature

Reporter Kurt Van der Dussen consulted state wildlife officials and an anthropologist from Indiana University in his efforts to discover what sort of creature was lurking around the Hardin Ridge Recreation Area in the Hoosier National Forest early in 2002. Even the experts were left scratching their heads, according to his February 1 article in Bloomington's *Herald-Times*.

Penny Howell and Dale Moore were just arriving at the home of friends who lived on Chapel Hill Road near the park's entrance in mid-afternoon in clear weather. But instead of being greeted by their friends, they found themselves staring at a five-foot tall creature covered in shaggy black fur. It glared back at them from a squatting position before ambling off into the woods on its hind legs. As it turned, Howell and Moore noticed strange white patches of fur on its head that stood in sharp contrast to the black. It left prints that were not those of the flat-footed hind feet of a bear or the giant feet of a Bigfoot. They resembled those of a large wolf or dog, with visible claw marks that rule out a great cat.

Howell and Moore were not the only ones to see the creature. The Web site BigfootEncounters.com reprinted another article of Van der Dussen's and one from the *Indianapolis Star* credited to the Associated Press that cited several other witnesses: Chapel Hill Drive resident Rick Deckard, and three customers at the nearby Hardin Ridge Store. All witnesses vigorously rejected arguments that they had seen some sort of escaped exotic animal such as an orangutan or rare species of bear. Deckard, who frequently bow-hunted in the woods, was also insistent that it was no bear or panther.

What was it, then? The closest exotic animal that I could find to the witness descriptions—and it is exotic, indeed —is a type of Madagascan woolly lemur, the indri. The largest lemur of Madagascar, the indri walks and stands upright and would appear about four feet tall standing up. (Prehistoric remains of lemurs show they once grew as large as great apes.) It has both black and white fur, but with much more white fur on its body than witnesses reported, and its monkey-like feet would not leave dog-like prints. The name lemur means "ghost," and the indri is credited with mysterious, magical powers by indigenous people of Madagascar.

I would say that the Hardin Ridge creature sounds more like a smallish upright canid than anything else. Many dog breeds have both black and white fur. As in the old saying about ducks, if it looks like dogman and walks like a dogman…

Westfield Werewolf

I received one other report from Indiana, this time from Westfield in the center of the state just six miles north of Indianapolis and a little south of the 1500-acre Morse Reservoir. Westfield lies in one of those fringe areas where cornfields mix with new developments, and the story involves another of those curious deer-sized canines. The witness, Pam, wrote:

"I had an interesting encounter in Westfield Indiana...It was a typical September evening in 2002. My daughter and I were coming home from the store around 9:00 p.m. when we saw something that looked like a large animal trotting in the other lane toward us.

"When we came upon it, we discovered it was a black, German shepherd-like dog about the size of a small deer, shaggy with clumps of hair missing. It was so unusual we circled and pursued. When we caught up we slowed and called to it.

"The animal turned and faced us in a rather challenging manner. It was at this point my daughter and I decided discretion was the better part of valor and left the creature to its rounds. No one in the family has ever seen the likes of such a beast before or since, but it remains a favorite topic at my daughter's sleepovers."

There have been other sightings in Indiana that I have omitted for one reason or another, but even more pop up in Ohio. Perhaps the Buckeye State owns an advantage in its generous Great Lakes frontage. And Ohio has had one real celebrity cryptid in the past decade.

Ohio Mandogs

The Ohio Mandog became a radio sensation in August, 2005, when a woman called in to *Coast to Coast AM* one evening to say that her boyfriend had recently seen what she called a mandog while driving his semi. Her boyfriend, Scott, testified that it reminded him of the were-wolf in the film released that same year called. They thought it might be related to an unidentified scream recorded near Liberty, a small town just west of Dayton and about six miles south of Sycamore State Park. According to an August 19 article in the *Cincinnati News*, however, an animal expert called in by the town said the noise did not come from any animal.

Liberty is in the southwestern part of Ohio, but it is a big state and sightings seem to come from all over. I will start with a report that came in on January 24, 2010, about a rather chilling incident farther north, in Mansfield, in November, 2008.

Mobile Home Mandogs with Crepitus?

Mansfield is easy to reach, lying about halfway between Columbus and Cleveland on Interstate 71. The thirty-nine-year-old woman who wrote me on Myspace.com said she was visiting her twin sister, who lives in a mobile home park surrounded by woods at the time of her sighting. Neither woman works outside the home; one is married to a truck driver and another to a US Postal Service employee.

One night during the visit, the sisters decided to take a little stroll around the park in the cool weather that hovered just above the freezing mark. As they rounded a corner on one of the lanes, the twins stopped short as a porch light from one of the homes revealed two black, dog-like creatures standing only about fifteen feet away from the road.

"They looked like dogs," she wrote, "but they were standing on their back legs like humans. I got scared and we ran back to the house. We got in the car and drove down to where we saw them and they were still there. When the car lights hit them, they ran off on their hind legs just like a human. They were creepy."

The creatures were totally black with tall, pointed ears, long snouts, and an appearance "somewhere between a German shepherd and a Doberman." She said the coats were shaggy with medium-length fur and that the front legs seemed shorter than the hind legs. "They never got down on all fours," she said, "but when they ran, their arms were sort of out in front of them."

She said that she did not notice any odor, but that the creatures made an odd "clicking" sound—although she could not tell whether it was coming from their mouths or feet. One was slightly smaller than the other, and they stood about five feet tall. Other people in the park have also reported seeing them.

The next day, the sisters walked to the wooded area again and this time heard the odd clicking noise coming from inside a huge brush pile, which they thought might be the canines' den. They decided not to disturb them further.

Are Clicks a Clue?

I must say that while I've received other reports of creatures that don't reach the standard six-foot height, the clicking sound was a new one to me. What animals "click?" Geckos. Sperm whales. Caribou click their leg tendons. Prowling cats will click their teeth at seeing prey. Anything with hooves will make a clatter on a hard surface. None of these animals match the twins' descriptions. And the animals' claws would not have clicked against soft ground as they ran into the woods.

Upon checking some veterinary websites, I discovered that dogs can make clicking noises in a variety of ways. Their leg tendons, like those of caribou, can return too rapidly when stretched, their joints can snap or pop just like those of humans, or clicking can also be a symptom of osteoarthritis as the bones grind against one another. If the sound originated from the mouth rather than the limbs, the clicks could be a sign of an elongated soft palate. This is a condition that occurs most often in breeds with shortened muzzles like pugs or Pekinese, but since the creatures the twins observed had long muzzles, that scenario doesn't seem likely. But several sources said clicking bones are a symptom of hip dysplasia, and the condition is called crepitus.

It seems logical to me that creatures not designed to walk upright might suffer bone, joint or tendon maladies like those listed above if they had indeed converted from four-footed to upright postures. So why they would continue to move bipedally, despite pain that makes them go clickety-clack?

Perhaps it meant that the bipedal posture was providing relief from bone spurs developed during their lifelong, four-footed posture. It seems logical to me. If humans must sit to relieve hip pain they have developed from overuse in an upright position, perhaps canines could get similar relief by doing the opposite: standing upright.

Large-breed canines are especially susceptible to hip problems. And in wolf packs, any member with a disability that might jeopardize the group's hunting success is cut from the pack and forced to go it alone. An animal with hip and back pain will not be able to hunt successfully by itself, either, and will probably gravitate to easier prey, such as carcasses killed by automobiles. That brings it to highways where it is seen standing up and munching dead deer or raccoons—and reported as a werewolf.

Eureka!

To find support for my theory, I contacted Professor Rolf Peterson of Michigan Technical University in Houghton, Michigan. For decades, Peterson has been studying a naturally isolated pack of wolves on Isle Royale, an island National Park in Lake Superior. The wolves have started to suffer from the effects of inbreeding, and that has given many of them back problems. Since Peterson and his associates observe the wolves through high-powered lenses from low-flying aircraft, I asked him if he had ever noticed any of them walking in an upright posture.

His answer was that he had not. He added, however, that while these wolves had diverse problems with their back vertebra, their hips all seemed to be perfect with no evident dysplasia. The upshot was that this was not a good sample population after all, since my hypothesis involved motivation from avoidance of hip pain.

Domesticated dogs and captive wolves are not good test populations, either, because they will continue to be fed and cared for whether they have hip pain or not. Without motivation to move, they simply lie still as much as possible. I have owned such a dog.

This was confirmed to me by Dr. Lois E. Bueler, author of a very useful book, *Wild Dogs of the World* (Stein and Day, N.Y., 1973). Responding to my email, she wrote, "I do not know of any reason why feral or wild canids would walk on their hind legs, and from what I know of canid anatomy they would not be (are not) very good at it.... The only breeds that seem even a little comfortable 'walking' on hind legs are a few of the small terriers. The hips, pelvis, and lumbar vertebrae of canids are not designed for bipedalism.

"In other words, anatomy tells the tale. In my experience, when dogs and wolves get arthritis (and they do get it, chronically) they slow down all their activities, stop running after short distances, resent external touch to their joints, and are extremely careful about posture. The virtually impossible posture of bipedalism would be the last thing they would engage in, I should think."

That would seem to shoot my theory in the paw. I do still wonder if perhaps it could explain at least a few sightings, especially those where witnesses have described the animal as looking "sad" or "starving." If true, it's no wonder these specimens are not attacking humans.

Akron Street Critter

Not far from Mansfield is the much larger town of Akron. A sixty-two-year-old woman wrote me in July, 2009, that she had seen an unidentifiable creature running across the street as she watched from her second-story window on a clear spring night that year.

"At first glance I thought it was someone that was running without clothes on. As it was getting closer, I saw that it was an animal. It ran on its hind legs, had the face of a rat, kangaroo, or any animal with those features, had extremely short fur, and stood over six feet tall."

The woman lives near the Akron zoo, and her first thought was that one of its animals had escaped, until she got a better look at it. After seeing it a second time, she is now afraid to go out in the parking lot of her building after dark, especially after she noticed a number of neighborhood dogs had gone missing. Her final message said that she had placed a camcorder near the window in hopes of capturing its image. I do hope she succeeds.

The woman had found me after hearing me on *Coast to Coast AM*—as did another Ohio resident named Tim, who wrote at about the same time, from that same northeastern quadrant of the state. He wrote about seeing a huge animal that looked like a wolf but was larger than a Great Dane as he and a friend sat on his grandfather's front porch in Cleveland. He was eighteen at the time. The animal was on all fours and walked right up and acted friendly, but spooked Tim and a friend when it continued to hang around and tried to get into the house through the doors and windows. His grandfather had just died, which probably added to the eeriness of the experience for Tim.

I received one more report from that same area (the listeners of that radio show are a mother lode of information) from someone who makes it his business to observe unusual things.

Portage County Razorback Dog

David Frost, from northeast Ohio in Portage County, runs the Center for Paranormal Research and Defense. On April 30, 2006, he wrote about something that he and his team experienced in 2004.

"We were on a patrol of a wooded area in mid-summer. It was about 12:30 a.m., give or take. We were driving a large Ford pickup truck. My friend and associate was driving, and we had two other partners in the back. The visibility was good, because it was a full moon. Had it not been, I don't know if we would have seen (the creature). I don't have much to go on (regarding) whether the lunar cycle plays any role, but coincidence or not, it was a full moon.

"We were approaching a hill. Next thing we know, this dog came running down the road toward us. It was on all fours and the biggest dog we have ever seen. As it approached it went and passed us on the driver's side. The dog's back came up to the middle of the truck window. So you can imagine the size of this thing. It turned around in the road and stood on two legs for a moment and then gave chase for less than sixty seconds. From there it went to the right and off into the woods. When it passed, its back was very…razor-like, I guess is a good word. Like the back of a hyena. All black hair, pointy ears, snout. Very dog/wolf-like. Thin and muscular. Not super long hair and not shaggy, but a good coat of hair nonetheless. That's all we saw."

The encounter spurred David and his group to keep making late-night patrols, and he wrote again on February 7, 2007, to say they had encountered what appeared to be the same the animal once more.

"We spotted the wolf-like creature again last night around 2:00 a.m. It was in the same area—same road—as seen before. The road we've seen it on is called Pioneer Trail. Before hand, we went down an adjoining road called Asbury. At the end of Asbury we found scattered deer tracks in the snow. It looked apparent, based on the tracks, that the deer was in a panic and all over the place. There were possibly more than one deer as well. But a few feet away we found much larger tracks, and they were bipedal. They were long and canine looking, but hard to tell.

"We went back down Pioneer Trail and stopped at the apple orchard. It's a whole field with row after row of apple trees. We spotted a deer standing idly. But in the row of trees behind the deer we saw a huge black mass. We backed the car up and we could see it. We could see its tail. It was very low to the ground and sniffing the air. It paid no attention to us this time. After a moment the deer ran off in the direction of Asbury. The creature pursued at a rapid pace and we lost it.

"Tonight we're going back out to look some more and we'll try to get pictures of the tracks for you to see, and if at all possible, pictures of the creature as well."

The pictures never arrived. But one more report makes me believe there is something huge in northeastern Ohio that is not your average Fido.

Norton Chicken Thief

A rural family near Norton, just west of Akron, has lived in fear of what's in their woods since March, 2010, when a dark creature emerged to snatch a rooster from their barnyard. The writer asked to be identified by just his first name, Drew, and said that he is a twenty-year-old, straight-A college student not known for causing trouble. His family's farm is near both a marsh and a cave system. He wrote:

"I've never really known much of the dogman, but have always been kind of a skeptic. I've heard of the Beast of Bray Road, overheard kids at high school talking about a supposed werewolf sighting nearby, and have seen Hollywood's spin on the dogman.

"Since my parents have lived here, about seven years now, we've all heard strange things. My mom and I have heard very distinct, VERY strange howls several times. I've heard many grunts and growls. I grew up in the country and I've always loved to hunt. I know what a lot of animals native to this area sound like and how to distinguish between them. I've never, even on television, heard anything like this. It sends chills down my spine when I hear it.

"About a month and a half ago, my mom told me a very strange story about the previous night. She had just gone to bed when she heard what she thought was me coming up the driveway. She thought it was odd, seeing as how she hadn't heard a car pull into the driveway. The footsteps came up the driveway until they were parallel with her window, which faces the driveway. She said that whatever it was dropped to four legs and ran VERY fast at her window. She immediately jumped out of bed in a panic, thinking that it was coming through the window. She told me that she would have written it off as a dream if her cat hadn't done the same thing that she did, but before she did.

"My parents have chickens. One of the roosters has been refusing to go into the coop because the other roosters have rejected it. My parents have allowed it to stay out at night only because it roosts where most animals can't get to it. I've had finals this past week, so I've stayed here for a nice quiet place to relax and study. I've been here all but one night that the rooster has been left out. I sit in my second story room on my laptop late into the night.

"Since the rooster has been out, I've heard something rustling around in the neighbors' yard in the plants on the opposite side of the fence just below my window across the side of my parents' yard (about 35 yards). It was very obviously walking on two feet. At first, I assumed that it was the elderly woman next door out for her nightly cigarette. I soon discredited that seeing as how it was after midnight and the sounds that came from the thing could not be made by any humans.

"As the thing wandered around back and forth along the fence, it seemed to growl and almost grunt. It was raining very hard, so I had to listen very closely. Whatever was moving around was the same thing as the previous night. It sounded very big. Eventually, the noises stopped and I went to sleep.

"The next day, I listened to the rustling again. After about a half hour, it ran very fast and I heard the leaves rustle like the thing jumped. I then heard a thump against the chicken coop, which sits next to the fence. The chickens inside began to cluck in a panic. Then I heard the rooster that was out clucking in a panic and it sounded like it was running around the yard. I heard grunts and growls following the bird. Then I heard a very vicious growl and the bird was silent. I heard the leaves rustle again like the thing leaped back over the fence into the neighbors' yard. I would like to note that it sounded like this thing took one single leap to cross the fence. The noise was like a single rush through the leaves. The rooster then began to make a noise that sounded as if it was in a lot of pain and being eaten.

"I grabbed my gun and a flashlight and ran downstairs and outside. I stopped just outside of the door, turned the light on, and pointed it and my gun in the direction of the noise. After scanning the fence line, I found the broken silhouette of the chicken. I saw the front and back parts of the bird, but there was a black spot that covered the middle third portion of the bird. I pointed the light at it and I could tell that I was looking (the creature) in the eyes. There was no reflection—I think this was because the eyes were out of the light. Whatever it was, it seemed to look through me. It turned my blood cold and I was paralyzed in fear. As I previously stated, I'm a hunter. That being said, I'm used to being in the wilderness and encountering bigger animals. Those animals don't scare me like this thing did.

"The thing then growled at me. Instead of walking toward it, I decided to get somebody to help me get the bird and/or capture this thing. My mom got up and I got dressed as she was getting her gun and putting on her robe. Before we went out, I told her that this thing is big and is undoubtedly bipedal. We walked out and my mom stopped when she saw the bag full of bread that my stepdad had left out to give to the chickens the next day. It was shredded, but all of the bread seemed to be there and none of the pieces were broken.

We then continued and I saw the full silhouette of the chicken. We walked closer and the bird was on the other side of the fence. At that point, I was assured that what I'd heard is what happened. I lifted the bottom of the fence so that the bird could return to our yard (there was no way that I was reaching over the fence). It seemed unharmed and ran straight under the porch.

"We took our dogs out to track whatever this thing is. They picked up the track and went to the fence, the coop, around the yard where I'd heard the thing chase the chicken, and then lost the track.

"After we went inside, my mom asked me if I ever return to my car after I get here at night I told her that I never do because I feel like something's watching me. She covered her mouth and shook her head. She then said, 'You're right. This thing is bipedal.'

"Apparently, she'd heard me come to the door at the top of the driveway. Then she'd heard what sounded like me walking back down the driveway almost immediately. She had gotten up to unlock the deadbolt so that I could get in, but saw me in the kitchen petting the dogs. She said that whatever it is either mimics my walk or walks just like me. She told me that I have a very distinctive walk…a no-nonsense, I'm getting where I'm headed walk. To me, this means that this thing has gotten very close to me without me even knowing it. As a hunter, I know how to listen for movement. This is shocking, disturbing, and downright scary.

"After going inside, we heard a blood-curdling howl. Our dogs would not leave our sides (a sign of protecting against danger) and were growling quietly until about 4:00 a.m.

"The following night, I stayed at a friend's house because it's closer to my college.

"The night after that, my stepdad was convinced that it was a possum. He wasn't home to witness the events of the night that my mom and I went outside. He stayed up until about ten-thirty to watch for this thing. I told him that it was too soon. At about 11:45, I heard the familiar howl from the direction of the marsh. I began to hear dogs barking in that direction also. The barking of dogs got closer and closer as time went on as if this thing was headed toward my parents' property.

"Again, after midnight, I heard the thing rustling around along the fence. I heard the leap again and the chicken was almost immediately making that painful cry. I ran downstairs and tried to wake my stepdad who had told me to get him if anything happened. He didn't wake up, but my mom heard me and came out with her gun. Once again, the bird was on the other side of the fence. Again, it seemed unharmed.

"I lifted the bottom of the fence and the bird ran through and headed straight for its shelter under the porch. My mom noticed that all but one of its tail feathers were gone. I would like to note that if this creature was as small as a possum or a raccoon, it would have been able to go under the porch after the chicken. The porch is only about a foot off of the ground at its highest point.

"Today we filled my stepdad in on what he'd missed. It seemed like the same thing over again. We took a walk in our friendly neighbors' yard and found the trail that I'd told them about. We also found broken sticks and plants in both places in which I'd placed the jumps. I found a print that was much bigger than my dogs', but the ground was wet and my stepdad had taken the dogs around there, so I can't be sure. The chicken is in a cage in our house to keep it safe from the beast.

"After these events began, I did a lot of research. I never actually saw the thing, but I'm positive that this beast is bipedal, at least my size (about 6' 2"), mean, and VERY agile. When I encountered this thing the first time, I got the feeling that it wanted to hurt me. After researching something that I've never believed in, I'm convinced that this thing is a dogman. (I'm still wondering why this thing didn't kill the chicken.) We've started escorting each other to and from our vehicles at night. Now, none of us will leave our house without some way to protect ourselves.

"I know that this isn't a coyote. I've never heard a coyote move like this thing. When it growled at me, I was sure that I was dealing with something out of the ordinary. Also, the fact that this thing walks on two legs is what made me research the dogman. From what I've read, I've kind of been waiting for it to just give up and go away. I'm hoping that that's what it will do. I really don't want to have to hunt something so rare and so different. I'm going to try to catch anything that I can on video and I've also been considering purchasing a scout camera that hunters use and putting it in the yard."

The thing that surprises me about this encounter—other than the ever-astonishing element of a giant, bipedal canine—is that the creature did not just make off with the rooster. It was already on the other side of the fence, and I cannot imagine that any wolf, coyote or feral dog would so easily give up its prize, especially not two nights in a row. Perhaps it was familiar with guns and feared that Drew might give chase and shoot it, but even that seems very uncanny behavior. It implies a level of thought able to handle cause and effect.

The other, far scarier, possibility is that the creature was baiting Drew with the rooster.

Wolves do use thoughtful strategies when hunting. In *The Company of Wolves* (Knopf, 1996), Peter Steinhart recounted a sheep farmer's experience with a pack of wolves that first attacked the goats which formed the nucleus of the flock. That way, the sheep would scatter and become more vulnerable to easy attack.

Steinhart writes, "We really know very little about what a wolf plans or thinks. However, those who spend time observing wolves see plenty of evidence that the mind of a wolf is complex, purposeful, and full of feeling."

The good people around Akron may want to blanket the area with game cameras...and lock all the roosters up tight.

Werewolves of Delphos and Other Ohio Legends

The small town of Delphos in the northwest part of Ohio had to overcome a daunting obstacle of nature—the Great Black Swamp—before it could be born in the mid-1800s. The nearly impenetrable swamp covered almost 5,000 acres along the Maumee River until settlers finally began to drain it to use as farmland around 1850. But according to *Delphos Herald* reporter Craig Adkins in a November 1, 2006 article, Delphos was a werewolf mecca in those pioneer days. Perhaps it was because their habitat, the swamp, was shrinking, but according to Adkins, the town's Resurrection Cemetery was said to have been overrun with dogmen. I would not recommend that anyone get too excited about looking for cryptids there, however. When I contacted Adkins for more details, he said that his article was based on old campfire tales that he had used (and embellished) when he was on a tight deadline for a Halloween tale.

(Strangely, another town named Delphos—in Kansas—was the site of "wolf girl" reports in 1974 when what looked like a blonde, female feral child was spotted around its environs.)

Reader Mark Bergman passed on the news of another early manwolf hotspot in Ohio. Only thirty miles north of Delphos, the city of Defiance also has a history of werewolves, according to *Creatures from the Outer Edge* by Jerome Coleman and Loren Coleman. In August 1972, people around Defiance and Toledo reported seeing a furry creature that ran upright, had a wolf's head with long muzzle and glowing eyes, and displayed an odd, side-to-side gait. Whatever it was had the ability to use tools, evidently, as a railroad worker claimed the creature battered him with a two-by-four.

I must add a shout-out to members of the Unknown Creature Spot Yahoo Group for digging up the original articles from the *Ohio Crescent-News* and the *Toledo Blade*. A *Crescent-News* story by Ellen Armstrong revealed that local police were armed with silver bullets and that citizens were in an uproar after a tall entity with a furry head and feet and *dressed in jeans and a dark shirt* acted aggressively toward several railroad workers near Fifth Street and the Norfolk and Western railroad tracks.

A second article in that paper chronicled two different residents "in hysterics" over the belief the "wolfman" was after them, even though neither had seen it. This article said the so-called wolfman wore some kind of animal mask, and that police were not sure of its motivation.

James Stegall of the *Blade* added that whatever the "creature" was, witnesses agreed it was "very hairy," and that even the police chief said there was "a lot of natural hair" in addition to the furry mask.

Although Armstrong's article said none of the incidents occurred under a full moon, Stegall reported that two railroad crewman said it had appeared under a full moon twice. From what I can deduce, the creature first appeared July 25 and then again July 30, and according to NASA, the full moon for July, 1972 occurred on the 26th. The crewmen were close, at least. And the sightings then ended.

Personally, I think the clothing is a fairly certain indication that this was a human hoaxer. If not, there are only three possibilities I can come up with:

1. The creature was an upright canine that allowed itself to be dressed in human clothing by a human (since its arms and paws could not manage buttons and zippers) and somehow was rigged up to be able to grasp and hit someone with a two-by-four despite lacking opposable thumbs.
2. The creature was a supernatural manifestation of some kind without limitations on appearances.
3. The creature was a tall story invented by railroad employees Ted Davis and Tom Jones.

Personally, I think someone in Defiance had a werewolf mask.

Port Isabel Pig-Ear

There is one more oldie to mention that is not so easy to explain.

Criss-crossing the state diagonally to the extreme southwest corner of Ohio—the same corner where the Liberty Mandog was reported—in the tiny berg of Port Isabel (about fifteen miles southeast of Cincinnati) two witnesses claimed to see a classic, transforming werewolf at a lover's lane while parking in 1964.

The story told in Leonard H. Stringfield's *Situation Red: The UFO Siege!*, described the couple's object of terror as a dark, six-foot-tall figure with glowing eyes that lunged at their windshield head-on. Transfixed by the hypnotic effect of its eyes, they watched as the animal form melted into a human one and then ran into the woods on all fours. They said it had fangs and "pig-like" ears, a description which sounds rather unlike a Bigfoot.

Reports of animal forms visibly morphing to human are rare, and I can see how the creature's movements could be misinterpreted by two startled people in the shadows of the spooky lane. Although it is possible the creature was a canine, I don't think there are enough details to identify it as one for sure. Maybe the town should change its name to "Pork" Isabel. (Again, via Mark Bergman).

Chapter 13

Kentucky K-9s

The Bluegrass State borders both Indiana and Ohio, with its biggest city, Louisville, lodged on the Ohio River just a quick swim south of the Indiana border. The state is very well-watered and forested, with many large pockets of secluded wild lands including the gigantic Daniel Boone National Forest. It's also in easy prowling range of that active southeastern corner of Ohio we just visited. Besides, it boasts a Wolfe County and town names like Black Snake, Flat Lick, Cranks, Cub Run, Quicksand, Raccoon and Dog Walk. You have to love such a state.

Best of all, in the 1770s a group of settlers established Kentucky's entire western half as a colony called Transylvania! A state studded with such colorful monikers simply must be inhabited by something more dangerous than thoroughbred racehorses. And by the accounts of some traumatized eyewitnesses, it is.

Beast of Bullitt County

Matt from Bullitt County, just south of Louisville, wrote me in August, 2009 about an experience his wife had there in 2005 when both of them were in high school. Bullitt County is home to the Bernheim Arboretum and Research Forest, 14,000 acres of woods that stretch into neighboring Nelson County. It teems with game animals, including wild turkeys, and is also the final resting place of the whiskey mogul couple who donated the whole shebang for public use.

Matt wrote, "I have some interesting things going on at the place I am currently living at. I met my wife in high school. In 2005 she came to school and explained to me that she saw a bear. We do not have bear or wolves for that matter in this part of the country. She described this thing she saw to me in detail, and I asked her if she was dreaming or on drugs! She is not nor never has been on drugs, and is a no-nonsense type of person. Her sincerity told me she was truthful in her story.

"She explained that she saw an upright canine in the driveway in rural Kentucky. It was nearly seven feet tall, with human-like hands, dog-like legs and feet. Head like a German shepherd's, and yellow eyes that reflected light. I have attached her sighting in detail to this email.

"When her family moved to this area, they brought with them cats, I think about three. There were stray cats that started coming around, and her stepmother is an animal lover, so she fed them. Cats do what cats do, and more and more cats came around or had kittens. I counted the cats, at one time there were 42 cats in their large back yard. I know that's a lot of cats. Some were friendly, some were wild and ran from you. Over the last four months that number has dropped to 19 cats. They disappear during the night, and there is no trace of them. No sound of a struggle, no fur, no blood. I have spent a considerable amount of time looking for any evidence of them with no avail.

"Along with the cats, there are dogs, four outside beagles and two inside beagles. The outside dogs are chained and kept together. During the night usually around two to three a.m. they will absolutely go off. It's crazy how distressed they get.

"I have heard deep groans/ moans down the adjacent hollows. Been outside and heard something big stepping on branches in the woods. I have heard this 'sniff' sound coming from the woods late at night that sounds like a dog stiffing the air. I have gotten feelings of something watching me at night. I have found paths where something of the same body size or bigger than me walked through a patch of woods, or a field. Also found strange, three-toed foot prints. They're large, but very strange.

"Based largely on the fact that my wife saw this thing once, and that cats are simply disappearing in the night without a trace, and the noises, feelings, and footprints, I think I may have some dogman activity going on. I work in public service in a high stress job. I am no stranger to fear. There is a chain across the driveway. And to get past the chain you must stop, get out, pull through, stop, and put the chain back. I work third shift so I must do this at night. I have my gun out every time, because I think something strange is in the area.

"I am in the process of getting a game camera that is motion activated, and I am going to place it in the spot I think this thing passes by nightly or almost nightly."

I haven't heard back from this gentleman, but I wonder how the farm's cat population is doing. They evidently taste very good to manwolves.

Land Between the Lakes

"I just heard you on *Coast to Coast AM*," wrote a man named Frank, "and the subject brought up some memories that I have never shared with anybody, but it made me start to wonder about things. I had a sighting about seven years ago at Land Between the Lakes National Recreation Area located in between Tennessee and Kentucky. I am not sure if you are familiar with it."

Actually, I am familiar with it. There is a well-publicized set of tales about that area of Livingston County published on the Internet and dramatized in a video, *Hunt the Dogman*, produced by Barton Nunnelly and Grendel Films, 2007. I'll give a brief account of those first.

According to Jan Thompson, the witness recorded on the film, her thirteen-year-old cousin was attacked and clawed in the leg by a large, upright dog-like creature in July, 1978. The seven-foot-tall, hairy creature followed the boy as he raced home on his motorbike, and it startled the family with a loud howl before showing itself at the end of the driveway. It broke a window in the terrified family's home before leaving. They learned that others had seen a similar creature at an old Boy Scout camp on nearby Kentucky Lake. There were also rumors of a family slaughtered by some unidentified predator at a nearby campground, but this has never been substantiated by any public record. The thirteen-year-old also glimpsed the beast both in the woods and staring into his house numerous times after his attack.

Author and investigator B.M. Nunnelly said in his book, *Mysterious Kentucky*, that Thompson described the creature as a "cross between the werewolf and Bigfoot," with a shorter snout, flattened ears and a big chest. (Reminds me of the Texas Snoutnose.) Frank's story involves something a little more to the canine side and, while it occurred more recently than Thompson's, it was still several years before the incidents portrayed in the Grendel Films video became widely known. Getting back to his story, he continued:

"A group of us had gone up there for the weekend. I don't know if the rest of the group encountered the animals or not; I never mentioned it to them for fear of being teased. We had all driven up to the campsite separately due to the fact that we all lived in different towns, and we met up nearby then drove out to the campsite. Well, we packed our trucks up and I stayed behind to make sure we left the campsite just as we had found it. I stayed for maybe another two hours burning off the extra fire wood we had gathered.

"It was dark by the time I left the campsite. I took the long way home going north along the trace road that goes down the center of the area. This area is very dangerous at night due to the large number of wildlife that is in the area. I was going about twenty-five mph. I remember all the white tail deer that were feeding almost in the road. After about twenty minutes I noticed that there weren't any deer where they had been just as thick as cows in a pasture earlier. I was maybe one hundred feet from the elk and bison prairie there.

"I noticed a group of deer run across the road so I kicked on the KC lights on my truck to see if I could see what was after them. I figured that dogs or another vehicle had spooked them. I didn't see anything so I kicked the off-road lights off and proceeded home. Then around 1,000 feet I stopped because there were deer in the middle of the road looking at something, and the fact that my truck was behind them didn't matter. They turned and darted after about fifteen seconds of me stopping. After seeing this I decided since there weren't any other cars coming I would drive with my off-road lights on till I hit the road to the Interstate.

"I hit my switch to turn on my lights and caught a glimpse of what I first thought was a rather large coyote. Until I realized it was running on its hind legs and just barely running with its front paws. I decided to pull up to where I saw it cross. With the amount of light my truck was giving off I could see a pretty good circle of area around me. I scanned the trees and grass to see if I could see the animal.

"I could see something moving back and forth in the tall grass but I couldn't make it out at first. It was moving back and forth edging closer to the truck till I could make out its grayish black fur and its snout. At this point three smaller animals ran in front of my truck the same way as the first one. I decided to turn my truck and aim my lights at the area and could see something standing in the grass around six and one-half feet tall maybe and three smaller ones walking back and forth near it.

"I decided to let my windows down and shut the engine off to see if I could hear anything. They were making sounds that I can best describe as the sounds that puppies make when they play but around three octaves lower. They weren't dogs though because they never fully put their weight on their front legs, they just kind of touched them to the ground when they paused to look at me. It's hard to explain but I could tell they didn't have normal paws in the front like a canine; they had more like a hand's appearance.

"I attempted to get my camera out of my bag but realized that there was no way my little point and shoot 35mm would get them in the picture; they were keeping just out of direct light of my truck. I finally came to the realization that this may be a mother and her pups. I have lived in the area around wild dogs and coyotes and the last thing you want is to get between a mother and her pups.

"I started my truck which startled them somewhat. The smaller ones ran off into the grass but the larger one moved closer just enough to bring its head and front legs out of the grass to where I could see. It had the look of a wolf but with much more fur almost like an Irish wolf hound. The eyes shined in the light like most wild animals…they had kind of a yellowish green glow to them. The ears were pointed back so I could not tell their exact position on the head. I decided to leave at this point; laid back ears are not a good sign. As I drove off it decided to let itself be heard. I could hear it plainly over my truck it was a very loud guttural howl sounding much like a wolf only a lot deeper and more raspy sounding.

"I don't know if you have had any sightings this far south. I don't know if these could be the same type creatures or not. After reading your site I can honestly say they were/are not a Bigfoot. They came nowhere to standing upright as a primate. When they ran across the road I could tell that the legs they ran on were like the rear legs of a dog but with more girth.

"I have yet to be back up there at night. I have yet to go back camping either. With as much wildlife as there is located there, not to mention they have reintroduced elk to the area, it could easily support a family of these creatures. I would really like to get your take on this subject because I really do feel like I saw something that isn't on a wildlife list of the LBL. These animals were clearly big enough to be the top of the food chain. Land Between the Lakes also has natural caves and numerous run down structures from different things that were located there. It would not be hard for these animals to find shelter well out of humanity's way."

Well, the flattened ears sound similar to the beast in Thompson's tale, as does the warning roar. It is possible they were the same creature, although Frank's sighting happened around 2002, about twenty-eight years after the thirteen-year-old boy's fright. But the creature Frank saw was evidently breeding!

Other witnesses have also reported seeing two or more creatures together; incidents in Rock County, Wisconsin and upstate New York come to mind. A few people have seen short, upright dog-like creatures that could be juveniles, such as the family near Freeport, Illinois. But this is the first report I've had of what sounds like a parent with pups. If these are indeed natural animals, however, dogman puppies would have to exist. The implications are sobering.

Nunnelly and fellow investigator Charlie Raymond started a website, KentuckyBigfoot.com, in 2005 to solicit and post reports of Bigfoot encounters in their state. They were not disappointed, but to their surprise they also began to receive messages from people who had seen things that sounded more canine than ape-like. Nunnelly covers these fully in his excellent book, but I will briefly summarize them here just to give some idea of what lurks where in the Bluegrass State:

More Sightings in Brief

1951, Henderson, western Kentucky on the Indiana border: five children and a woman saw a man-sized, wolf-like creature peering into the living room window of a home on Wilson Station Road. It had pointed ears, a muzzle, shaggy fur and wore a tattered, filthy white shirt.

1975, Boyd County, eastern Kentucky: a woman driving on Rte. 168 saw a six-foot-tall, shaggy-furred creature with long snout and fangs. She also noted a sense of temporal displacement, as time seemed to "slow down" when she passed the creature, although fright can sometimes distort our perception of time.

1980s, Boyd County: Ashland Kentucky Cemetery was said to be frequented by a wolf-like creature that could run on two or four feet, leap easily over high fences and chase people—including two policemen —in a taunting manner, before running away. (This behavior is consistent with most manwolf reports.)

1991, Harrison County in eastern Kentucky: two people driving on a gravel road outside Cynthiana saw a three-foot creature (juvenile?) run across the road on two canine-like legs.

Early 2000s, Greenup County in eastern Kentucky; a couple driving separate cars home at night were stunned when a "werewolf-looking thing" covered in fur, with pointed ears and long claws, ran at each of their cars and vaulted over them before running into the woods.

March 1, 2005 around 5:00 a.m. in rural western Bullitt County, a woman encountered a six-to-seven foot tall creature walking upright about forty yards away in her driveway. It had a well-muscled chest, canine head and legs, dark fur, and turned its head to look at her when she gasped before it darted into the trees on two legs. Its eyes reflected yellow from a nearby security light and it had ears similar to a German shepherd's. Her family had noticed many cats gone missing around that time.

October 3, 2009, Beattyville: a young man in a tree stand saw a six-to-eight-foot upright creature with a face like a wolf and dark fur staring at him, yellow-eyed, from only twenty yards away.

None of those sound like Bigfoot to me.

Chapter 14

Yes, Virginias, There is a Manwolf

Kentucky's eastern border is bounded by Virginia and West Virginia, and both states seem to have been visited by manwolves.

A reader called my attention to this item from *West Virginia Ghost Stories* (wvghosts.com) titled "Demon Creature." It almost perfectly describes a classic manwolf. The site owners gave me permission to reprint it here, and as in other quoted accounts, I have edited slightly for spelling and grammar.

"My brother and my father have seen a creature in the counties to the south of Charleston, which is best described as a 'demon creature.' I myself have never seen it, and I was having trouble believing the stories until I saw a story on Discovery Channel about a 'demon creature' that has been spotted numerous times in Connecticut. The encounters they depicted on this show matched exactly to what my dad and brother had told me about years ago.

"My brother and his fiancée were walking up the mountain behind my grandmother's house in Yawkey, West Virginia in the spring of 1980. Since the peak of the mountain offered a spectacular view, he was wanting to propose to her there. As they were walking up a narrow trail at about three or four in the afternoon, they heard what sounded like a bear coming up towards them from the left side of the trail. The mountain had thick underbrush on both sides of the trail, so they were unable to see exactly what it was until it stepped onto the trail approximately twenty to thirty feet in front of them.

"My brother has hunted all of his life and is familiar with all of the indigenous species in these woods, but he says that he has never seen anything like what stood before them that day. It was a large, black-furred animal that was much larger than a bear, and had a long bushy tail and pointed snout similar to a wolf. When it first stepped on the trail it was walking on all fours. My brother says that it had a foul odor, and the very sight of it made his hair stand on end.

"At first it seemed as if the creature was unaware that they were even there, so they stayed completely quiet as my brother eased his fiancée behind him in a feeble attempt to protect her in case this thing attacked. When it stepped on the trail it suddenly came to a stop, stood up on its hind legs like a man, and then turned and stared at them. My brother says its eyes were small and shone bright neon red.

"When it stood on its hind legs, he said that it easily stood seven feet tall. His heart sank when it turned and looked at them—he knew for sure that they were dead. But then it walked off the very steep side of the mountain to the right of the trail, still standing on its hind legs. He says that it didn't stand like a bear, but almost as if it was meant to be walking on its hind legs, which were somewhat larger and longer than its front arms or legs.

"After recounting this to my father, who had grown-up in West Virginia throughout the 1930s and 40s, he said that he knew of this creature from when he was a child. He said that it would come around their home occasionally and kill some of the livestock. The thing that scared him the most about the creature though, was the fact that their dogs were scared of it and would crawl as far under the house as they could get whenever it would come near. Apparently these dogs weren't afraid of anything except this creature.

"He said that when it would walk around the house at night, you could see the top of its back extending well above the window sills, which were already several feet above the ground, and could feel the ground shudder with each step that it took. As it would approach, a foul odor would fill the house. Then, the next morning, they would find where it had killed a horse, or cow, or other such livestock. To this day nobody has ever been able to tell exactly what this thing is, but many have reported having encounters with it."

The site owners told me they never received any more information on this sighting, but the fact that the same type of creature has been seen for decades in that area probably means it is not a single, natural animal. The long, pointed snout and bushy tail rule out Bigfoot or bear. Whether it is truly a demon is anyone's guess.

Something Amiss in Amissville

Investigator Scott Marlowe of PangeaInstitute.us sent this report after receiving it from a radio listener in June, 2009. The woman, named Ruth, told about a "bizarre, wolf-like creature" she and a friend saw around 2004 on Rte. 17 in Amissville, west of Warrenton, in early autumn. She wrote:

"We may have seen it twice.

"Anyway, we were on our way to a friend's house about 9:00 p.m. that night. It was very dark by this time. No discernible moon. We turned off to the left at the old post office (whatever road that is) and drove a mile or two. I was driving. To the left, I saw a huge, black, what appeared to be a calf-sized rottweiler by the side of the road in some tall grass. Its eyes were glowing red in the headlights.

"I pulled to the right side of the road to stop and call it to me to see if it had tags (I have large dogs and do volunteer work for a shepherd rescue group.) But my friend yelled, 'Don't get out—I don't think that's a dog! We're late, anyway.' When I looked back for the creature, it had vanished into the tall grass and woods. We continued on to our friend's house a few miles down the road and told her what we'd seen and our friend said that the whole area seemed really creepy at night.

"On the way back, we slowed down to look for the dog again, but saw nothing out of the ordinary—a couple of rabbits; an opossum. By the old post office, we turned back onto Route 17 towards Midland and drove down the four lane highway. We'd only gone a few miles. We were driving slowly, because there are usually lots of deer out at night. The four lanes are divided by a wide, grassy and sometimes hilly median strip. There were no other cars on the road at that time as the area was much less developed back then. The road was dark most of the way, but we had just passed a small roadside diner to our right. It was closed, and the parking lot was empty, but that section of the road was illuminated by street lights.

"Suddenly, about thirty feet in front of us—no more than that—a huge black wolf-like creature crossed diagonally in front of us. We both saw it clearly. It was moving in the oddest manner with a camel-like motion. It had a definite, triangular wolf-shaped head with pointed ears and snout, but much broader. Large, visible canines. Its head and neck were set very low into the shoulders, and its back sloped slightly downward, similar to a hyena, but it was much broader, and more massive all over, bigger than a large mastiff, and it was a solid black color, not brindled or mottled. The tail was full and long like a wolf's. Hair about three or so inches long, longer on the shoulders.

"It was definitely not a black bear; I've seen plenty of bear on Skyline Drive. The shape and floating gait were all wrong, and it had definite canid legs and paws. It easily weighed 200 lbs. and did not look like any wolf or wolf-hybrid I've ever seen. In fact, something seemed very wrong and out of place about the whole thing. Almost as if a creature like that shouldn't exist in this time. And that we were meant to pay attention to something.

"Anyway, we circled back at the next turnoff, but the werewolf (can't think of a better description)—or whatever it was—was gone. My friend and I both saw it and remember all the details. It's etched in our memories. We've both told other people, and of course, our husbands, but only a few people believe us. But we know that we both saw it. We're in our early fifties, now, and hadn't even had a glass of wine that memorable night. I'm glad other people have seen similar things. I guess there's room for everything in this universe. I did find Linda Godfrey's site, later, but the creature I saw was not bipedal, nor did have hand-like front paws."

The counties surrounding our nation's capital have long been known for sightings of goatmen, but this seems to be another of those pesky giant black dogs that just strike people as "wrong." I will be discussing those later in Part Five.

Chapter 15

Maryland Monstrosities

Yipes, Stripes!

Moving on to Maryland, a man who at the time of his sighting was 23 or 24 and had just received a degree in biology gave me this unusual report; he now holds a doctorate in aquaculture and fisheries and makes his living in that field. He wrote:

"This sighting occurred in late fall of 1976 in Frederick County, Maryland, near the town of Thurmont. My friend had picked me up at my house and we had gone into town with plans to meet some other friends to drink some beers at a local pub. Since our friends had not yet arrived, we decided to take a short drive up Rt. 77 to a field where it was common to observe deer feeding at night.

"The field was on the edge of the woods which bordered the areas of the Cunningham Falls State Park and the Catoctin Mt. National Park. We drove off the main road onto a small private access road which led up to the field. Upon arriving we drove the car to a point where the headlights illuminated the area, but to our disappointment, no deer were to be seen. After spending several minutes there we turned the car around and slowly headed back down the small road from where we had entered.

"Suddenly from the left side of the road a large creature, running on two legs, bounded and leaped across the road and disappeared into the brush on the other side. It passed directly in front of us, not more than

30 feet away. My first reaction was shock and amazement, but I quickly controlled my surprise and decided not to say anything to see if my friend would react and allow me to better determine what had just happened. Immediately he exclaimed, 'WHAT WAS THAT MAN!!!' In a calm but excited voice I replied, 'Tell me what you saw, tell me what you saw!'

"We both began to describe to each other the strange sight which had just passed before our eyes. Here I wish to add something that is hard to explain except to those who have had a similar experience. When one sees something that is totally unlike anything one has seen before, it is actually hard to put into words or even cognitively recognize what that thing is or what you have seen. It is hard to get a point of reference for something unlike anything you have seen before. Thus we spent the next couple of minutes trying to calm down and decide just what it was we had seen. Needless to say we were both nervous and a little shaken from the experience and decided to continue directly back to town.

"Both of us had a good look at the creature. It was likely at least 6 ft tall but inclined forward since it was moving quickly. Its head was fairly large and similar to the profile of a wolf. The body was covered in brown or brindle colored fur, but the lower half had a striped pattern of noticeable darker and lighter banding. The forelegs (or arms) were slimmer and held out in front as it moved. The back legs were very muscled and thick similar to perhaps a kangaroo.

"I do not recall the tail of the animal, although my opinion is that it did have one. It moved in a leaping bounding motion and crossed the distance of the road in front of us in two or three leaps. It was very fast and athletic and was obviously trying to get away quickly. This was not a hominoid type creature; it did not have the characteristics of an ape. It was much more similar to a wolf or ferocious dog, however it was definitely moving upright and appeared to be adapted for that type of mobility. I was particularly impressed by the size and strength of the back legs, the stripes on the lower half of the body and the canine-wolf-like head.

"After we calmed down, my friend and I talked about whether or not we should report what we had seen, but we decided not to. I mentioned to him that years previously in the mid sixties there had been reports published in the local paper the *Frederick News-Post* of some hunters who had reported a similar creature in the Frederick Co. area. At that time they called the creature a 'duwayo' (I am not sure the spelling is correct). Because of this we decided this is what we had seen.

"That evening we told our friends the story, but they weren't too inclined to believe us unless they could see it for themselves and we were definitely not interested in going back to the area that evening. Since that time I have moved away from the area and have had only a few opportunities to see my friend who shared this experience with me. Every time we've met, however, he always asks me if I remember the night we saw the duwayo."

The "duwayo," more commonly spelled "dwayyo" or "dwayo," is a name from the first decades of the twentieth century in Maryland, used for a tall, furry creature most often described as either bear-like or resembling what we might now call Bigfoot. The creature was said to live in Gambrill State Park in Frederick County in the 1920s. But later reports from the 60s claimed the creature was black-furred and, according to Matt Lake in *Weird Maryland*, "dog-shaped."

I could not find any older reports describing a wolf-like biped with striped hindquarters, however. The stripes made me think of the thylacine (a marsupial—not canine—native to Australia but thought extinct since the last one died in a Hobart zoo in 1936) and also certain striped hyenas, but the witness insists the animal he saw was neither.

"The animal we saw was nothing like these (thylacines or hyenas) in its totality. It was big and definitely bipedal, at least at that moment," said the witness after I asked him about the possibility. He did say that it more closely resembled my "indigenous dogman" sketch, although with larger, more muscular legs.

Interestingly, author Joan Dixon says in *Fauna of Australia* that the thylacine could bound like a kangaroo on its hind legs when it wanted to. It could also stand upright with its soles flat to the ground by balancing with its tail, and a film exists that shows a captive animal doing this.

The National Zoo in Washington, D.C. did boast a female thylacine or "Tasmanian Tiger" and three cubs from 1902-1905. One cub died soon after arrival, the mother died in 1904, another cub (male) died in 1905. A surviving daughter was mated unsuccessfully to an imported male. All of these animals, according to an article from the Smithsonian, have been preserved by that institute; therefore, none could have escaped to form a wild, relict population in Maryland. (It is remotely possible that a private collector could have had some, since the animals were being widely hunted and trapped in Tasmania at that time.)

Many believe the carnivorous animal, which is about the size of a smallish gray wolf on average (though larger specimens have been recorded), still exists in the wild on Tasmania. Much has been written on that subject and the creature's possible continued existence, but to date there is no conclusive proof.

This is the first time anyone has reported to me an upright, bipedal, wolf-like animal with a striped lower body. I agree with the witness that although it was highly unlikely that he saw a Tasmanian Tiger, his report was fascinating nonetheless. I'd be interested if anyone knows of similar incidents in that area of Maryland, which has had its share of odd critter reports, such as the goat man I mentioned earlier.

Some thirty-three years after this witness' encounter, it is probably not possible to determine exactly what he and his friend saw that day. But due to his education and vocation, the witness seems very qualified to describe an unknown animal, and although I doubt that relict thylacines could explain most U.S. sightings, I felt his experience was unusual enough that it deserved to be shared. He does not want publicity, but his identity is known to me and checks out. I will let him have the last word.

"Like I said before, this is something that happened years ago but was real, and I have never forgotten it. I don't want to be creating any new issues, simply want to add an anecdote to your credible case histories. I support the work you are doing, and I hope one day some of these mysteries can be solved."

Elkton Entity

East of the above sighting, near the Delaware border in Elkton, Maryland, a couple was driving home around midnight one evening in 2004 on Old Field Point Road. They were enjoying their quiet ride on the wooded country lane when a pair of glowing, greenish eyes flashed in the headlights.

"At first I thought (it) to be a deer standing at the side of the road, because of how high from the ground the eyes were. Not wanting to hit it, I slowed down, and upon closer inspection, realized it wasn't a deer. I thought it was a large dog, just sitting there. As we came up closer, we could see that it was hunched over on its two hind legs with its arms out in front of it, almost as though it were eating or holding something. It had furry finger-like paws.

"It was covered with brown fur, very scruffy and mangy. It was a darker brown, but not so dark as to be confused with black. Its fur at the back of its neck was very wild and appeared longer. Somewhat like a dog when it's riled up. It had the face of a dog, with a sort of snout-like nose and pointy ears. It happened to be sitting next to a mailbox. Now, the man that lived there had a very long driveway and he drove a full size truck. He had a taller than average mailbox so that he could just pull up and easily get his mail without getting out of his truck. This thing was sitting taller than the mailbox. I would estimate it to be about six-feet-tall or even a few inches taller, when standing.

"That is when I was one hundred percent sure that it was definitely NOT a dog. I have worked around animals my whole life and owned, worked with and trained all sorts of dog breeds. This was no dog that I have ever seen. Honestly, it looked like a werewolf.

"As we had approached it in our vehicle, my husband and I stopped our conversation as both of us were wondering what in the world this thing could be. I sped up because it frightened me. It didn't make any move at us; it just simply watched our car go by. As we passed it my husband turned to me and said, 'Did you just see what I just saw?' We were both very alarmed, and when we got home we quickly closed the garage door. We told our kids and their friends about it because, honestly, we lived perhaps a half a mile from where we saw it so I didn't want them going anywhere near the woods to play.

"About a year later, my sister-in-law's best friend described seeing the exact same thing one night coming home from work. It was dark out but not really late. She lived on the same road and it was in the same area that we had seen it. She said that its back was turned to her and as her car approached it, it turned and she saw its face. It looked the same, except this one ran off.

"Now, she said that when it ran, it ran on its two hind legs, but somewhat hunched over. We had never told her about our sighting, and when she described it to me I got chills because she was describing the exact same creature that we had seen. I know that it sounds insane, and most people might call me crazy, but I would swear that this creature was a werewolf like the ones you see in the movies.

"I know what I saw, and my husband has also said the same thing. It made me think how many urban legends and such are really based on fact. I wondered how many other people have seen this creature. I will upload a copy of the drawing my husband did of it if you'd like. He used it to show the friend and see if that was indeed the creature she had seen. She said yes."

The sighting just described was quite a bit later than the 1976 sighting, and doesn't sound at all like the striped creature seen in Frederick County, but they both qualify as extremely unknown canines.

Chapter 16

Scary Home Alabama

Alabama is one of those quintessential southern states people have always written songs about; there is even a famous southern rock group that uses its name as their own. It is understandable. Many rivers run through it as well as the huge Talladega National Forest. It was on a river near Selma that one of the most memorable manwolf encounters I've ever heard nearly did in a local fisherman.

Roaring on the River

I received two emails from a fifty-six-year-old man named Kerry in August, 2007, and I also interviewed him by phone on August 5 of that year. I will leave this largely in his words:

"I've never told this story to anyone. I could hardly believe it myself, so I thought it best to keep it to myself for the same reason most others keep theirs secret. This took place near Selma, Alabama on the Alabama River. Selma is located a little north of Montgomery, the state capitol. It's a lonely little river with hardly any homes built on or near its banks. There's some barge traffic moving timber to the paper mills, but that's about it. It's also an area that was inhabited by the Creek Nation, and there is also a lot of arrowheads and shards of pottery to be found. It's south of where I live, and the name of the launch is called Bogacheta.

"It has some good fishing for largemouth bass, which is why I used to go there, and was what I was doing when I was confronted by this fearsome critter. I remember it was late May or early June, 1981 or '82 and I was jigger-poling for bass. It was dusk and I was trolling the banks of one of the many little ponds or small lakes that branch off the main river. I was by myself—well almost. I had Sarge, my male pit bull, with me because of the local 'wildlife' that were subject to rob you at the isolated little boat launch on this part of the river. He was attack-trained by me, I used to train dogs for the police and he was the devil's lap dog, you can believe that! I had a seventeen-foot Grumman boat.

"I got to the launch about 6:00 p.m. and had just enough time to get to where I wanted to run my jigger pole before it got too dark to see where I was going. This river is very narrow and has shallow sand bars that you can cross over into large lakes (for lack of a better term). These lakes open up and are covered with lily pads and grass, perfect for jigger-poling!

"To give you an idea of what I was doing, I'll explain. Jigger-poling is using a long (eighteen-foot) pole with a twelve-inch line on it and a top water plug. You tap the end of the pole in the water to simulate a bait fish school retreating from a game fish. You move it in and out of the lily pads and hope some big ol' bass will hit the plug. At any rate you have to have your bow up close to the back as you troll the length of the bank. When the fish hits you just stop trolling and pull your catch in.

"We were coming down this bank and I had caught a nice bass. When you fish this way it's top water action. Lots of splashing by the fish; they make quite a commotion, plus Sarge was doing his thing barking and growling at the fish, quite a sight in itself. So I take the fish off and start moving down the bank, I must have traveled a good seventy yards down the bank and Sarge started putting up quite a fuss. The hair on his back was standing up and he would bare his teeth and snarl. He was on point and ready.

"I thought he was just overly excited about the fish and didn't really give it much thought, when all of a sudden it came rushing out of thick growth on the bank and into plain view. I was, and I mean this, terror stricken by the sight before my eyes. This fella was huge, that's right I said fella. I saw his pod!

"All I can say about it is that it was big and ugly. He was hunched over slightly, he could have easily been six and one-half to seven feet in height. With reddish dark brown hair or fur (that part is a little dim). He had a long snout full of teeth bared all the way back and he was really raising hell back at Sarge. The head is what I remember most, and it was big and dog-shaped, but it wasn't dog-shaped, if that makes any sense. It had a forehead like a human and it drooled and slung the saliva every-where. It had large yellowish green eyes, and pointed ears that were laid back, like a horse that is mad. Its chest was very muscular and didn't have as much fur or hair on it as the rest of it. I didn't see its legs hard-ly at all. And it was standing on two legs. Its forepaws were short and kinda stuck out in front of it, with claws. I didn't see a tail on it either. There was this rancid smell in the air as well, that added to my horror.

"All this took place so fast, but it seemed in slow motion. He was no more than ten feet from my boat. He was standing knee deep in water, and moving toward me. I threw my pole down and moved to the back of the boat and started my motor, all the while trying to get my pis-tol out of my bag under the console.

"Sarge, meanwhile, had gone to the bow and I thought he was going to attack the (expletive), I was fearful he would get killed so I slammed the boat in reverse and backed away. As I was backing away he stopped his advance, must have been the motor, I don't know. He whipped around and headed for the bank only a couple of feet away. Just as he set foot on the bank I opened fire with several rounds, I was so scared I'm not sure if I hit him or not. The whole event was full of the most ungodly sounds I ever heard.

"Now this thing was standing on two legs. That above all was the part that made me think I was losing my freaking mind—I know in my mind this can't be possible but me and Ol' Sarge saw it big as life. I've never been back there and I wouldn't go back there for love or money! There's no doubt that he heard us and was stalking us and meant to harm us. It's so clear in my memory it's like it happened yesterday. I don't drink and I don't do drugs...never have! Since I was a child I have been a fisherman. I don't get to fish much now because of my health, but I have been fishing rivers and lakes in these parts for a long time."

Kerry's phone interview version of his encounter was consistent with his account above, and I thought that he seemed both sincere and still sure of what he saw. He did expand on his description of the crea-ture in reply to my questions.

"This guy wasn't a bear," he said. "I could see its hide or flesh. Its hair was two inches long but I could see musculature and rib cage. The shoulders were narrow, not broad like a man's and slanted upwards. Its ears were long but laid back like a dog or horse that gets mad. The hair on its head was longer. Drool was just flying; he was on kill mode."

Kerry said it did make a growling sound which he described as "Argh, argh—that 'A' sound, real throaty. It didn't sound friendly to me."

It also had a noticeable odor which Kerry said smelled like "old dog pee in carpet, smelly, musky, like urine."

He did not know whether he hit it with any of his bullets because, although he emptied the nine-shot clip, the creature did not yelp or cry out.

"To see something like that out of the blue is unnerving as hell," Kerry told me. "I was always embarrassed to say anything about it because it's so outlandish. I've tried to convince myself that I didn't see it, but I know it wasn't a hallucination. What I saw is what I saw. It was flesh and blood."

Geographically, Selma and the big river that laps at its heart lie less than ten miles south of the Talladega National Forest with its plentiful game. Selma also has some interesting historical connections beyond the famous Civil Rights incidents that occurred there in 1965. Local tradition has it that Selma is the site where Spanish explorer Hernando de Soto met sovereign Mississippian chief Tuskaloosa in the mid-1500s, before embarking on a war that killed a great many Mississippian people in various villages along the Alabama River. Kerry told me that the launch where he liked to fish was known as a good place to find arrowheads and old pottery, so it is not impossible that this area was the scene of something more horrendous than a manwolf attack almost five centuries ago.

Perhaps the carnage left a permanent imprint.

Selma lies about thirty-five miles west of Montgomery. Forty-five miles northeast of Montgomery, sandwiched between the eastern lands of the Talladega National Forest and the massive waterways of Martin Lake on State Hwy 22 is Alexander City. Fifty miles south of Montgomery, maybe a two-hour drive from Selma, is the small town of Luverne. Alexander City and Luverne have something else in common with Selma besides proximity to Montgomery. They are each a site of an unknown canine encounter.

Quadruped: The Beast of Emuckfaw Creek

In late December, 2009, a nineteen-year-old man I'll call Steven wrote me about a creature witnessed by him and his parents on November 1 of that year, around six or seven p.m. on a clear night with full moon. They were driving home from Roanoke and were just about to cross the Emuckfaw Creek Bridge on State Hwy 22. His mother slowed down the car to look at an animal that she and his father saw illuminated in their headlights as it crossed the road.

"I looked up too late and only saw the back part of the animal," Steven wrote, "but my mom and dad got the best look. They said it had a long snout and its bottom canines were sticking out. The creature's front legs were smaller than its hind legs, and it had big paws. As for the ears my parents don't remember what it looked like. I only saw the back part of the animal but the headlight hit its fur just right...its fur was black, red and silver. Its tail was like a wolf and its paws were big. It was no coyote since it was much bigger than a coyote. I would say it was bigger than a wolf; it looked kinda muscular to us. My mom and dad say the closest size they can think of would be a big German shepherd.

"There are woods on both sides of the road. The oddest thing was the animal just walked across the road. My mom and dad said it was creepy but for me, I was fascinated that I had the honor of witnessing maybe an undiscovered species of animal. We didn't feel like the creature was going to harm us in any way...my dad thought it might have been a chupacabras since some people say the chupacabras could be some kind of canine. For now I'm calling the creature I saw the Beast of Emuckfaw Creek."

Emuckfaw Creek, by the way, is the site of a historic battle in the Creek War of 1812-1813 that was fought between two factions of the Creek Nation and the Tennessee Militia under Andrew Jackson.

Carcass of Ivy Creek School

A much older incident said to have occurred near Luverne, Crenshaw County, is like no other I have ever received. It dates back to the autumn of 1945 or 1946, on the grounds of a rural school built in the 1930s. At that time the former student, who wrote down his recollections for me and also granted a phone interview, lived only a quarter mile east of the three-room school on Ivy Creek Road. What he remembers, an unexplainable carcass and a howl that spooked a whole community, is remarkable. He gave me permission to print his original text:

"The discovery was on a weekday morning as it wasn't there when school ended the day prior to its being found. This school building was built in the late 1930s and is still standing. It is a long building with two front entrances with covered porches and the usual steps up to the entrances. A highway instead of a dirt road is the road in front of the school today. This was an extremely rural area at the time and the present population is at least triple what it was then and many houses have been built since then.

"My memory was refreshed about this incident by a friend sending me a picture (I believe the pic was drawn by Linda G.) of a creature that was from a story featured on *Coast to Coast AM.* about a creature referred to as Dogman of Michigan. After recovering from the shock of seeing an almost replica of the creature I viewed in the schoolyard those many years ago, my memory was jogged to the point that I experienced cold chills with standing hairs on my arms.

"Of course, my creature was only part of the upper torso of the creature. It looked to be part human, part dog with hands, arms similar to human. Its head was shaped somewhat similar to human but the nose was somewhat like a pug dog with the canine teeth. I can't recall the ears or eyes, but believe them to have been similar to human.

"The carcass was covered with fairly long hair, even the entire face had the same hair except shorter. Of course, we kids (I was ten to eleven years old at that time) kept getting closer and closer to the creature. The teachers, whom I still remember by name, ordered us back into the school house. I remember the complete absence of any blood.

"Some of the older neighbors came to view this creature after word got around about its existence. Not one knew what kind of animal it might be.

"The arms and shoulder area were similar to human but it had no discernible neck. The hands were similar to human with much shorter fingers with claws instead of fingernails. Of course we kids were worried that there may have been more of them and some may have been still alive.

"It stayed in the yard all that day and I believe until the middle of the next day before being disposed of. Memory of what happened to it escapes me. I have not been able to find anyone who remembers it or if any pictures were taken of the grisly find. The problems with finding people who remember the incident are; the older citizens of the time have since passed on and the younger ones were still in the military due to World War II.

"The howling/screaming incident happened one night either that week or the next. My mom, my brother and I were home alone not long after dark and we heard what I would describe a cross between a howl from coyote or wolf and the scream of a panther or catamount. It was scary to us. As it came closer to our house, from the direction of the school, we decided it would be in our best interest to leave.

"We walked with purpose to a nearby neighbor's house about three hundred yards down the dirt road. We and the neighbors could still hear the screams even that far away. It finally hushed. A short time later, we saw dad's car pull into the yard and went back home. As dad was eating supper, we were telling our tale and he was pooh-poohing the idea. Well, about that time this thing cut loose with a blood curdling scream that sounded like it was under the house!

"Needless to say, that got Dad's attention and he got a lantern and out we went to find the critter or whatever was making that noise. Once outside with the lantern and looking under the house, the critter screamed again but this scream seemed to come from the top of the house. We never found the source of the sound. Once or twice more during the night the scream was heard but seemed to be further away. The areas under and around the house were well searched the next morning and not one out of place track or other evidence of the incident was discovered.

"The neighbors who heard the scream seemed to think that it was a critter looking for its friend that was killed in some manner and left in the schoolyard. I think night travel was curtailed in the area for a few weeks after these incidents.

"The biggest mystery to me is how the creature got into the schoolyard in its found condition. Obviously, it died or was killed somewhere else as there was no blood in evidence. It has been a long time since these incidents. I've never forgotten the incidents and these words, to the best of my recollection, are exactly what I experienced."

The gentleman told me that he remembered the creature as if it were yesterday. He agreed that the fact that so much of it was missing made it even harder to identify, and I have to say that it seems to have had much more human-like characteristics than your average dogman. The description of human-like ears, shoulders and hands but no neck sounds very like Bigfoot, but the snout and clawed "short fingers" reek of dogman. The feet, had they been present, would have told the tale.

I did contact the editor of the *Luverne Journal*, hoping that someone would have written an account from an adult's perspective and that—hope against hope—someone else might have brought a camera. So far nothing has turned up.

Chapter 17

Northeastern Unknowns

Hunting the American Werewolf featured sparse sightings in the northeastern area of the US, mainly the jogging canine duo glimpsed running along the Interstate in upstate New York by two brothers in 2004. While I still would not call the region America's upright canine hotspot, there seems to be a slowly accumulating body of sightings beyond the eastern reaches of the Great Lakes.

Some reports are a bit thin; one man wrote that he has seen a pack of large, reddish dogs that look like hyenas and run very swiftly on Interstate 91 near Holyoke, Massachusetts. He claimed to have seen one take down a deer with a single bite to the neck. I have to put this one with the unknown quadrupeds.

Maine Jeep Attacker

A researcher I met at Fort Fest in Baltimore in 2008, Jim Boyd, shared a report he received a few months later in October of an encounter in Dover-Foxcroft, Maine. A woman employed as a supervisor at a local company was running some late-night errands and had just placed some items inside the passenger door of her Jeep when something growled from the dumpster behind her. She immediately ran to the driver's side and had just hopped in when she felt something push "violently" against the other side of her vehicle. The "something," to her great shock, was a six-foot-tall canine with a muzzle, stringy hair, a slim build and hunched back. It reportedly left claw marks on the roof of her Jeep.

New Jersey Unknowns

New Jersey comes up as the northeastern sightings winner. I chronicled only one northwestern New Jersey sighting in *The Beast of Bray Road*: a woman vacationing at Mountain Lake in Warren County in 1985 saw an upright canine running across the road with a deer in its forelimbs. But a friend recently pointed me to a pile of reports in the *Weird New Jersey* (www.weirdnj.com) magazines, particularly issues twenty-five and twenty-six. These magazines are written and edited by mavens of weirdness Mark Sceurman and Mark Moran, who also co-founded the *Weird US* book series. It's such a surprising clump of incidents that I'll offer a brief rundown of each, with permission of Sceurman and Moran.

The first occurred somewhere in the Jersey Pine Barrens, a vast tract of more than one million acres of pine and oak forests stretched across seven counties in New Jersey's southern half. The Pine Barrens, of course, are better known for the mysterious creature dubbed the Jersey Devil, which has been described as everything from a gargoyle to a winged kangaroo. There was a huge and hysterical flap of Jersey Devil sightings in 1909, especially in Haddon Heights, with sporadic reports of the monster coming in to present times.

This unknown canine sighting, however, did not include a date or exact location. It was from a woman named Cecelia Downs who said she was driving through the Pine Barrens around 2:00 a.m. when she saw what she thought was a bear on the side of the road. When she got closer, she realized it was not a bear but something that looked more like a "dark-colored sheepdog" with red, glowing eyes. As she slowed down for a better look, it rose on its hind legs to face her standing up. "Not the way a dog does," she said, "but like it was able to walk on its hind legs." She reacted in the way most such witnesses do; she stepped on the gas and left the creature to walk the Pine Barrens ditches by itself.

The other four sightings and legends mentioned in *Weird New Jersey* all occurred on the eastern side of the state's northern half.

Megan Reilly retold a legend of Howell, a city about fifteen miles from the Atlantic Ocean and about an hour's drive south of Perth Amboy. The creepy tale Megan had heard since childhood concerned a "devil dog" wolf-dog hybrid that haunted the woods around Howell and Ramtown along the Metedeconk River in the early twentieth century. It was alleged to have killed both people and farm animals and was given the eerie name of Bloodvulle (or Bloodville?). According to the legend, it was caught and chained to a tree where a subdivision now stands—and can still be heard howling at night.

The other three sightings occurred in the highly populated areas just west of the Hudson. One came from a female E.M.T. named Carla who wrote that her E.M.T. boyfriend had a very wild experience as he and his partner returned to Bayonne from Jersey City after transporting a patient late one moonlit night.

He had taken a turnpike ramp off Montgomery Street when he spied what looked like a very oversized, muscular black dog with longer fur at the base of the neck, long legs and yellow eyes walking calmly across the road in front of him. While this creature was not strutting bipedally, I have to mention that sightings at on-off highway ramps seem to be another of those recurring themes in unknown canine sightings. After all, given today's long stretches of unbroken four-and-six-lane highways, where else is a flesh and blood creature to dash for its roadkill—or a fay entity to cause mischief?

Another truly odd quadruped was reported by Brett Omelianuk, a motorcyclist driving along U.S. Hwy 202 between Oakland and Wayne about thirty miles south of the Wanaque Wildlife Area, near Pompton Lake. He had slowed down to enjoy a view of the full moon when something far more startling came into his line of sight only a few feet away on the road ahead of him. It was a white-furred, extremely muscular creature that ambled leisurely on four legs as it regarded him with what he described as "jaundiced eyes."

It stood nearly four feet tall at the shoulder, he said, and its musculature was clearly visible as it walked.

The creature's head was by far its weirdest part. Omelianuk said it was oversized and human-like—no specifics given—with a ruff or mane, a feature I hear about frequently in witness descriptions. He emphasized that he had a very good look at the creature since he was so close to it and he was on a cycle rather than inside a car. The animal continued on its way into the woods on the opposite side of the road, and Omelianuk kept going his own way. He added, surprisingly, that he later saw the same creature on two other occasions, by Pompton Falls and on U.S. Route 46.

Thanks to Mark and Mark at Weird New Jersey for their permission on the recap.

Modern Church Grime of East Hanover

The final weirdo of New Jersey that I'll mention here, a mysterious biped in a sort of churchyard, appeared in East Hanover as three eighteen-year-olds walked home from a restaurant. The writer, Mike, said they had not been drinking. As they passed a large parking lot in front of a church, they noticed a lone figure in the lot that they thought might be a reclining deer. As they moved closer to investigate, the "deer" looked at them, and they noticed it had large ears on top of its head. Thinking it was perhaps some wounded animal in need of rescue, they tried talking soothingly as they approached it. At a distance of about forty-five feet, the creature suddenly leaped to its feet—its hind feet only—and ran off into a wooded area on two legs. Mike said its arms swung as it ran, reminding them of an ape despite its dog-like head. The three young men ran the other way, screaming.

Modern-day crossroads, churchyards and beasts of the ancient forests—sounds like New Jersey is medieval Europe all over again. And this has not been an all-inclusive tour of the northeastern U.S. by any means. But since I am constrained by the limits of paper and print, I will move on to recent revelations from the state where the manwolf phenomenon first became widely known—Wisconsin.

PART FOUR

Wisconsin: Unknown Canine Central

Although I hope that by now I've demonstrated the depth and breadth of the upright canine conundrum across the continental U.S., I still am confounded by the wealth of sightings in Wisconsin. The reason may well be the simple fact that I live here; therefore, more people know I'm collecting reports. All the Bray Road hoopla and publicity may be another factor—although a large percentage of witnesses say they were not aware of those reports before their own sightings. Wisconsin, however, boasts a bountiful supply of all the features that seem to attract or go hand-in-paw with manwolf sightings: lake and river systems (especially proximity to the Great Lakes); plentiful woodlands; cornfields; and ancient, sacred sites.

Chapter 18

The Bearwolf of Holy Hill

Probably the most publicized Wisconsin sighting in the past decade is the one I have dubbed the Holy Hill Bearwolf, which occurred across the road from a famous shrine north of Milwaukee in Hubertus on November 9, 2006. The Roman Catholic shrine known as Holy Hill—with twin spires that are lit to gleam against the night sky—has been a landmark for years on its hilltop setting. It sits just west of Glacier Hills County Park and overlooks two river systems, hilly woods, and marshes. Rural subdivisions dot the area along lanes with names like Troll Hill and Hogsback Road. And local legend says the area has been haunted by a murderous goatman since Civil War days.

The Spires of Holy Hill

Two things beside the sensational nature of the 2006 sighting probably contributed to the media frenzy that ensued: one was that the witness, thirty-nine-year-old Steven Krueger, was a contractor for the Wisconsin Department of Natural Resources. The other was that Krueger reported his experience to the local authorities, which meant that his report went straight to the media via the sheriff's event log.

Krueger had a regular patrol route and normally worked with a list of pre-tagged deer assigned for pickup. He came across a small carcass too freshly hit to be on his list that night at about 1:30 a.m. on the shoulder of State Hwy 167. After throwing the deer in the back of his pickup truck, Krueger still had to document it so he climbed back in his cab and began filling out paperwork. He left the truck bed light on as well as the flashing amber light atop the cab and the interior cab bulb—so his immediate area was well lit.

As Krueger sat at his work, he felt his whole truck rock. He shrugged it off as the wind until the truck rocked a second time, even harder. Krueger glanced into the big side mirror on his truck door and stared at a creature covered in dark fur. It stood upright as it reached into the truck bed with one extended paw, grabbing at the deer. Its head was like a wolf's, Krueger said, with a long muzzle and pointed ears on top of its head, but it seemed thicker in the neck and body, reminding him somewhat—but not exactly—of a bear. As he realized he could not recognize the creature that stood six to seven feet tall behind his truck, the avid outdoorsman went into shock for a few moments. Then he stepped on the gas.

As he drove away, he heard two things hit the pavement, and he knew what each thump represented. One was the deer he had just taken, and the other was a metal ATV ramp Krueger used to slide larger deer into the truck. It had been lying just under the deer, and he surmised that as the creature pulled the deer out the ramp came with it accidentally.

Krueger drove for several miles, meeting no other traffic, until he came to an intersection and paused for a few minutes. As he recovered from the fright, he decided that the ramp was worth risking a return to the scene and headed back to retrieve it. Although less than ten minutes had passed by the time he reached the spot, there was no sign of the deer, the ramp, or the creature.

Figuring the public should know there was a possibly dangerous, large animal on the loose, Krueger next drove to the Washington County Sheriff's Department in West Bend and filed a report. As soon as the recording deputy heard the description of an upright, furry creature, he wrote down the very inappropriate word "yeti," thereby inspiring the local TV stations and newspapers to call it a Bigfoot sighting. To this day Krueger refutes that term for what he saw. Although he shunned appearances on local television, he did consent to tell his story on camera several years later for two History Channel shows, *MonsterQuest* and *The Real Wolfman*, and for a segment on Fox News Channel's *Sean Hannity Show* in July, 2009.

Interestingly, Krueger had a second sighting of what he thought might have been the same creature—but on four legs—in June, 2007.

He wrote, "I was picking up a deer on the north side of Zedler between Parkside and Thornapple in Mequon. As I was loading the deer with my winch I glanced up and saw the VERY large wolf come out of the brush from the north side of Zedler and head south down Thornapple. It was walking casual and I don't even know if it saw me, if it did I was no concern to it. Its back was about four feet from the ground almost touching the bottoms of the mailboxes. Its fur was pretty dark. It was by far the biggest wolf I've ever seen. I did not know they got as huge as that one was. I called the DNR and they confirmed that wolves have been known to travel the lake down from up north, but also there are people that have wolf hybrids as pets."

Was it a wolf that Krueger saw both times? Perhaps, but Krueger plainly saw the deer-napper reach into the truck to grab the deer with its paw. Although wolves do sometimes use their forepaws to hold onto prey, more typical canine behavior would be for the animal to support itself with its forepaws while lunging for the carcass with its jaws. And I've often noted that, other than for occasional reports of noticeable

Spot across from Holy Hill where Steve Krueger saw the creature

shoulders and elongated paws, the main difference between manwolves and very large timber wolves seems to be mostly behavioral.

Manwolves have also been observed holding prey with their paws while walking on their hind legs or while "kneeling." Witnesses have also noted that the forepaws seem to have longer "fingers" than is normal on a canine paw. Another important fact is that these creatures have also been seen many times converting from bipedal locomotion to moving on all fours, and vice versa. Therefore, I can't rule out the possibility that the June sighting may have been the same creature Krueger saw earlier, but in a quadruped position. It may also have been a grey wolf passing through the area. There is just no way to know.

More Bearwolf Buzz

Krueger was not the only person to discover evidence of an unholy terror in the Holy Hill area. The day after Krueger's 2006 sighting, a local hunter and business owner named Mike Lane heard the news reports and looked around the area for footprints, thinking he would see huge, Bigfoot-type tracks—since that was what the media had reported. Instead, he found deep, rounded prints consistent with a large canine—except they were made by a biped. The tracks went through a boggy field and disappeared into a marsh very near Krueger's encounter. They were too indistinct to make casts or a definite identification because of the soft mud, said Lane.

Author's interpretation of canine with thicker torso nicknamed Bearwolf

Lane also reported hearing about a secondhand sighting on Oct. 25, 2007, near Krueger's original incident. A local man told Lane his brother was driving along Hwy 175 near midnight when he saw something big running along the adjacent railroad tracks, clearly distinguishable by moonlight. At first, he thought it was a bear because he estimated its weight at about 300 pounds and the creature was running on four feet. Then he realized it did not move like a bear and it looked more like a large dog. Then the "bear" stood up and began to run on two legs, and the man realized it was no bear. Bears will rear up sometimes to see better, but they do not normally run on their hind legs (with the exception of one famous 3-limbed sow with cubs shown on YouTube in spring, 2010). This creature, though, continued bipedally at a rapid pace.

Painting contractor Rick Selcherk told Milwaukee WISN TV reporters that in 2004, he witnessed a very large, upright creature crossing Slinger Road, just south of State Hwy 60, near a railroad and part of the Kettle Moraine State Forest. The area also includes a forested riverway that leads to the Holy Hill area. The creature "shifted its weight strangely on its hind legs," he said, and he was not able to identify it as anything he had ever seen.

It was dark-furred with long tufts on its chest and legs, said Selcherk, and it had a round head with a snout and dog-like, pointed ears on top. However, Selcherk said its legs were more like those of a bear than a canine. In *Strange Wisconsin*, Selcherk said, "It was nothing close to a deer, but it didn't really look like a bear. It looked like a weird combination of two animals." It had a short, wide tail, he added.

I was also contacted by a man who was driving with a friend on Shalom Drive, off State Hwy 144 northeast of West Bend on November 12, 2006, when a deer-sized creature that was not a deer crossed the road in front of them. It had a wolf-like, pointy-eared head and a canine body but was too large to be a wolf and too lean to be a bear.

Another man who wanted to stay anonymous said that around 1996, he and his employee were returning home at about two a.m. on Scenic Road, only a quarter mile from Holy Hill Road, when they saw two upright, hairy and fast creatures crossing the road near a cemetery. They were seven feet tall and had "slanted eyes." The men agreed not to talk about it, as they felt no one would believe them. I did not hear from the man again, and it's hard to say just what the creatures were, given the description. But they were obviously not known, recognizable animals.

Something just as odd was spotted near Watertown, about fifty miles southwest of West Bend, by two co-workers driving home late one night around 2005 on Navan Road. They were traveling in separate cars, but each saw the same thing. They described it as a large, strange creature walking in a hunched position on its hind legs with the help of one front limb, as if one of the hind legs was hurt. It was so tall that its head was taller than the first person's SUV as it crossed the road right in front of her. Its fur was dark, shaggy and matted, they said.

Heard But Not Seen

Another report from Washington County came from a woman named Sarah, now a fifty-seven-year-old California resident, who wrote me in May, 2006. It was not a visual sighting, but I include it because the incident supports the possibility of a large predator in the area, and because it is one of the better examples of many letters I receive detailing frightening howls, growls, and footfalls in the woods.

"Let me start off by telling you how grateful I am that you are compiling this information on the werewolves of southeastern Wisconsin. Hearing about your book jarred my memory about an experience that I had more than thirty years ago as a teen living in that area.

"We were a group of around five or six friends and family (all older teens) who were camping overnight at a private campground on a small lake in the Kettle Moraine State Forest region of Washington County, Wisconsin. The year was approximately 1970, in midsummer. The nearest town was Kewaskum. It was very rural farmland mixed with deciduous and pine forests. We chose to relocate our campsite a little bit further from the main campground in a secluded, natural, practically circular, clearing. We liked this spot because of the unusual shape and the fact that it contained a sort of carved-out depression in the center. Here we wished to build a fire and hang out. The sun began to set.

"As we built our fire, roasting hot dog's and singing, someone happened to remark upon the primordial setting and how we resembled a group of ancient peoples who may have done just what we were doing thousands of years ago. Time passed and the hour was 10 p.m. or so and we began to exchange spooky stories. The sky was very clear and there was an abundance of shooting stars. Also, the moon was so bright we could actually see quite a bit although we were far from any city lights. Everything grew very quiet. There were crickets, of course, but no other folks were around—only us.

"Suddenly from off in the woods we heard the sound of something coming toward us, breathing heavily. This area had long ago become devoid of any large wild animals. Pieces of wood were crackling and breaking as it walked. We could hear large, trudging footsteps in the underbrush and a loud, snarling, huffing, puffing breathing sound. It did not sound like an animal, but more human. Soon we also heard twigs snapping and the creature, whatever it was, getting closer and closer to the edge of the woods and near our clearing. It let out several bloodcurdling growls and was so close we were terrified. That was all it took for us to be so shaken that we gathered up all of our gear and ran out of there as fast as we could so the creature could not get us. It really was trying to chase us out of its spot, I believe. None of us slept the entire night.

"I have been in camping situations where young men try to scare you, but they are usually in groups or drunk and end up showing themselves and causing trouble. This was one creature against several of us and it showed no fear.

"I am sorry to say that we did not get a glimpse. At that time everyone knew about Bigfoot so we assumed that is what we had encountered. We talked about it but never found out what was out there until I heard of your research. Could this possibly have been the man-dog? Could we have accidentally conjured something up due to our youth or presence in that particular place?"

I wish that I had good answers for Sarah's questions. It could have been an upright canine, but we will never know for sure. I think "accidental conjuring" is less likely. But who know what kinds of spirits live in these dark woods? I should mention that Lizard Mound County Park, a site of ancient effigy mounds, lies just a few miles to the southeast of Kewaskum, as does the Shalom Drive bearwolf site.

And perhaps ten miles to the southeast of that Kewaskum area campground is the little town of Newberg. A man who requested I withhold his name wrote about another incident...

Manwolf Mini-Me

"In late summer of 1987, I was dating my now ex-wife and was driving her home to Newburg from Jackson (note: ten miles south of West Bend). She lived on the outskirts of town in an old farmhouse, and we were on a side road.

"It was late at night when we spotted an animal on the side of the road. As we were approaching closer to the animal it looked at the headlights and then ran off into the field on two legs. The animal had a head that is best described as dog-like and it had been feeding on a road kill. I am for certain it was only about three feet tall, not the six or seven that other people have reported.

"I stopped the car and wanted to go after the animal and Laura was adamant that I did not. I was raised hunting and had spent a lot of time in the woods and had never, and have not since, seen anything like it. I have always wondered through the years what this animal actually was and then just probably four years ago I saw a television program regarding the Wisconsin Dogman. I told my girlfriend that I had once seen it years back but that it was smaller than what most people were describing it as and of course she thought that I was pulling her chain. I guess the only reason I am even contacting someone now, is that I bought her *Weird Wisconsin* book and saw the link for Linda Godfrey on the back inside of the cover."

There are other supporting reports worth a mention, such as a Fond du Lac business owner who saw an upright creature with a "wolf-shaped head" near Hwy 60, west of Hartford, in 2000. More recently, four men saw a dark-furred, bipedal creature walking near Holy Hill just before ten p.m. March 7, 2007. Only a month earlier, in February, 2007, an unrelated person wrote that he and a friend saw something lying on its side on a highway median near West Bend that appeared too large to be a coyote but too lean to be a bear. It had brown fur and was gone by the time he returned later in the day.

Sightings of the creature in Washington County seem to have calmed down in the past two years, at least as far as I know, so perhaps it has moved on or retreated into the wilder areas of the Kettle Moraine State Forest's northern unit. As for Steve Krueger, he has since stopped contracting with the DNR for health reasons and is now a self-syndicated cartoonist of a feature called Moose Lake. (He does not draw werewolves.)

Chapter 19

More Milwaukee Area Monsters

I've noted a few Milwaukee area sightings in past books, such as Kim Del Rio's childhood encounter in *The Beast of Bray Road* and the *Hunting the American Werewolf* story of the teen girls who stopped on a Brookfield highway on-ramp to aid what they thought was a lost dog—until it stood up. But there have been many other sightings in the Milwaukee and southeastern Wisconsin areas, perhaps because of their proximity to Lake Michigan.

Lake Michigan Manwolf

People often ask whether I make on-site investigations of reports. I do—when doing so makes sense. On Saturday, June 30, 2007, I received a call from several people regarding the sighting of a bipedal Manwolf that fulfilled all my requirements for a road trip. It was recent (June 26, 2007), on accessible land, within reasonable driving distance, and occurred in weather that might permit evidence to remain. In addition, there were three young adult witnesses who swore they had not been drinking or doing drugs previous to the sighting. On top of all that, there was a full moon.

The site, Fitzsimmons Road, runs east-west between South Milwaukee and Racine. It is partly closed off by a barrier just after a few residential blocks because at the end of its one mile length, it crumbles off into an eroded cliff over Lake Michigan. Because of that, the road has a longtime reputation as a lover's lane, haunted by the spirits of teens whose cars supposedly tumbled over the edge. The witnesses had been lured to the road by hopes of seeing a phantom '57 Chevy when they set off on foot about 1:00 a.m. the night of June 26, their way lit by a three-quarter moon and a streetlight.

The group consisted of Jonathan Hart, then twenty-five, and Jonathan's brother Benjamin Hart, then eighteen, plus a twenty-two-year-old friend of Jon's that I will call Jane and two eighteen-year-old friends of Ben's, Breonna and Shawna (last names withheld). As they proceeded down the dark lane, they all heard a high-pitched, drawn out scream coming from somewhere in the cornfield to the north of the road. (To the south was a wheat field.) It sounded like a woman, said Jane, yet they knew it was not human.

They had walked about half the length of the road and were still next to the cornfield and about one-eighth mile from a small wooded area that leads to the cliff, when Ben spotted a pair of almond, yellowish eyes glaring at them from the brush. That was all his two friends, Breonna and Shawna, needed to convince them to return to the car. They retreated speedily.

Jane, Ben and Jon were curious enough to remain. Jane trained her flashlight on the eyes, which appeared to belong to some kind of furry,

View of cliff overlooking Lake Michigan at the end of Fitzsimmons Road

canid creature crouching on all fours at least forty feet away. To their amazement it rose onto its hind legs and faced them in a menacing pose.

Its chest and stomach area were light tan, with its dog-like legs and forelimbs and face a darker "clay" brown, said Jane. Its fur was shaggy. Ben, who stands over six feet tall, said the creature was as tall—or taller—than he was. The creature then moved one forelimb as if getting ready to come toward them, and the three humans shrieked and ran. Ben was in the lead, followed by Jane and then Jon. They could hear the animal's feet hitting the ground with the weight and rhythm of a biped, but faster than a human's feet would go, they said. It closed the distance between them in seconds, and they felt it could easily have caught them had it wanted to.

At one point, the creature did catch up to Jon, close enough that he could feel its body heat and that he "felt its presence," as Jon put it. The creature grazed the back of his shirt with the tips of its claws, leaving two sets of triple 5/8" slashes about one inch apart on the back of his cotton, button-front, over-sized *Cheech and Chong Up in Smoke* shirt. Jon said that he felt warm at the point where his shirt was touched, but the rest of his body felt cold, "goose-bumpy and shivery." His skin was not scratched.

He kept going. At a short distance before they reached the barrier and street light, they no longer heard the footsteps. The creature had vanished back into the cornfield. The three terrified young people joined the two girls already in the car and left.

All during the chase, they said, they kept hearing the same type of scream they'd heard at first in the field, but lower-pitched and "more aggressive." They could not tell as they ran whether the sound was coming from the field or from the creature chasing them. As they ran, Jane said, she turned several times to turn her flashlight on Jon and the creature to make sure Jon was still there and could glimpse the dark form behind him.

Once inside their car, they sped away and went to the Hart home where they told the two brothers' mom about the incident. Their mother told me later that her eighteen-year-old sobbed as he related the story and that he was truly frightened. Their mother's sister was the one who finally contacted me.

The witnesses were all positive this was not a bear, human in a suit, or Bigfoot, based on what they saw and how it moved. Jane said it was "human-like in shape but deformed or hunched over…. It walked on its toes like a dog, not flat-footed." And Jon said that he could smell it behind him and it had the odor of a "dirty critter."

Author's photo of tracks found in mudhole in wooded field off Fitzsimmons Road a few days after sighting

"Ever since then we've been on edge," said Jane. "It's not an experience I'd wish on anyone."

"I wish I hadn't been chased by it," said Jon. "It felt like we were running for our lives."

When I arrived at the scene a few days later, I walked the length of the road with Ben, Jon, their mother, aunt, and Jane in bright daylight. We found some canine prints on the sand point at the end of the road that measured about three inches long and could have belonged to a large dog, but not to a wolf-like creature that stood six feet tall.

As we walked back down the road, we took time to investigate a few paths and tractor lanes that led off the road. Off a deer trail into the woods on the north side of the road, we found a clay-mud water hole covered with animal tracks. There were prints from what looked like some larger type of canid mixed with numerous deer prints and a few prints identical to the three-inch prints we found earlier at the end of the road. The larger prints measured about eight inches long and showed claw marks.

It looked like some predator had ambushed a deer; the deer's prints angled deeply into the edge of the clay where it apparently had sprung away.

Could the canine prints really have been that large? Sometimes footprints left in mud will spread and widen as the mud settles out, creating falsely large tracks, but in this case, the other animal impressions made a handy source for comparison. Since the three-inch prints were identical in size to the others found in the cliff sand, and the deer prints also measured a normal size, it was unlikely that only the eight-inch prints spread in size.

I emailed a photo of the larger print to a Department of Natural Resources wolf ecologist, Adrian Wydeven, and he agreed that the larger print looked like some type of canine had made it. He added that sometimes wolves will walk in such a way that their hind feet step exactly in line with the front paws, making the prints appear larger, but my own view is it doesn't look as if that is the case here (see photos).

The other possible evidence was the clawed shirt, which Jon gave to me for several months in case I found anyone equipped to analyze it. The two sets of tears were very clean, however, with no detectable residue of any kind. It did seem to me that an animal lunging forward might have exerted enough force to have completely shredded the shirt down to the bottom, but Jon said he never felt the claws on his skin and felt the creature barely touched the shirt as it billowed from his body while he ran. He later noticed a slightly raised red mark on one arm but told me he didn't think it had anything to do with the creature.

A few of my blog readers have suggested that Jon's "Cheech and Chong" shirt, with all its implications, makes this whole case suspect. I asked Jon about that shirt connection several times, and he has maintained that his clothing choice was incidental—he bought the shirt for its humor—and that he and the others were cold sober that night.

The fact that the brothers' mother and aunt vouched for the boys' account of the events and also accompanied them when we examined the site did give me more confidence in their report. The late Janesville filmmaker John Gage also told me he felt they were truthful after he filmed—and grilled—them a year after the sighting for a documentary video he was working on at the time.

I conducted another phone interview with Jon Hart on April 19, 2010, and he reaffirmed all of his prior statements. "It was there," he said. "I can still picture it in my mind clear as day. It's totally inexplicable."

Rainbow Park's Golden-Eyed Beast

It was in the same general range of time, either 2006 or 2007, that Judith Halverson, then in her late fifties and a customer records clerk for a major southeast Wisconsin retailer, also saw a similar creature just south of Milwaukee. The incident occurred in the parking lot of Rainbow Park, just north of the Root River Parkway in the West Allis area. It was near midnight on October 31—she is not sure of the year—and she was on her way home from a late night snack run to a nearby George Webb.

Of course, the mention of Halloween is always a big orange flag, and so the first thing I asked was whether she might have seen someone in a costume. She convinced me otherwise in a phone interview, after a relative asked her to call me.

She stopped at the park that night, she said, because it had a big trash can in the parking area and, for reasons of her own, she wanted to dispose of her hamburger wrappings. She got out of her car, walked the few steps to the container and was preparing to get back in her car when something came running at her on all fours from very close by. It was only about twenty-five feet away, she said, when to her great surprise, it stood up.

"Its eyes were gold," she said, "and it looked at me with a sort of grin; it didn't look like it was going to hurt me. It had ears, pointed, on top of its head like a dog's but its head looked more like a wolf. It was not a dog and it was not a costume. It wasn't skinny—not straggly or starving—but it was taller than me, I'm five-foot-two, even though it was hunched over. It was on its toe pads; it was not a Bigfoot. Its body was like a Husky or bigger dog with a wide chest and long fur." She described its color as "the color of a deer, beige."

She added that she was sure it was all animal, saying, "I didn't see any man-look on it. It wasn't a face like a human's, the teeth were jagged."

Furthermore, she witnessed the creature opening its mouth to bare its muzzle-full of jagged teeth as it stood up, an action that a mask (outside of some very sophisticated animatronics technology) would not be able to replicate. It did not make any sound, and she did not notice an odor.

One point that Judith kept emphasizing was the golden color of the creature's eyes. She said that although the only light in the parking lot was not shining directly at the creature, the eyes glowed and looked bigger than normal. The eyes impressed her as "evil," even though she did not feel the creature would hurt her.

"I'm sixty-two now," she said, "and I've never seen anything like that. I've seen timber wolves and they have green-gold eyes. I know what I saw."

After the creature stood up and "grinned," it kept walking into the brush on two legs as Judith hurriedly got back in her car and left.

Judith told me she has never seen any other "weird things" in her life, and she felt this was a solid, flesh-and-blood creature. She called one male friend to tell him about it and he laughed, so she stopped talking about it except to a few relatives.

Although Judith believed that the eye color—actually the color of the animal's reflective membrane called the *tapetum lucidum*, or "bright carpet"—was highly unusual, I think that it does fall within the general color range of yellow or yellow green normally exhibited by wolves. Yellow-gold is a possible eye shine color for dogs, too. And an animal's eye color can also affect the color of its eyeshine.

I've mentioned this before, but great apes, including humans (and presumably Bigfoot), have no *tapetum lucidum*, and therefore no true eye shine. A human's eye may look red in a photo lit with flash, because the flash reflects off the eye's capillary-rich retina. But a creature with eyes reflecting bright gold is not likely to be a human in a gorilla suit.

Incidentally, these facts about eyeshine also leave me at a loss to explain the occasional sightings of creatures, usually believed by witnesses to be Bigfoot or black canines, with eyes that appear to glow red. Owls have red or orange eyeshine and forward-facing eyes but lack big furry bodies. I will hop aboard that train of thought in the next section of this book.

The eyes, it seems, do not always have it.

Chapter 20

More Southern Wisconsin Encounters

Pleasant Prairie Pond Beast

The very pleasant village of Pleasant Prairie lies in the extreme southeastern corner of Wisconsin and is known to archaeologists as the site of some of the state's earliest Native American habitation, with ancient campgrounds dotting its eastern edges. With such an innocuous name, it hardly seems appropriate to think this little Kenosha County area may shelter a manwolf. The following letter from "Jason" argues otherwise.

"I had a strange encounter with an animal of some sorts in 1983," the witness wrote. "I was fifteen years old, and me and my friend Charles decided we were going to camp out in some woods by a farmer's pond in Pleasant Prairie. I was familiar with this area from hunting there. There was some in-laws of my brother who lived close by so if anything happened we could go there.

"My father dropped us off and we fished the pond that evening and fell asleep that night—nothing unusual happened. The next morning we got up and were fishing the pond again. I started to walk around the corner of the pond and there standing by the pond was the strangest looking animal I have ever seen. It was about six-foot long with dark brown fur, it had dog-like characteristics but was not a dog—it was very large. I stood maybe ten feet away from it. It was staring at me, and I was staring at it.

"In one quick move it went off through the woods moving so quickly and gracefully it was amazing. My friend Charles never saw it. I was in shock at what I had seen. Needless to say, I left right away. I told my dad what I had seen and he looked at me like I was nuts. Needless to say after that look I didn't speak of it again. I went home and looked at every animal book—it resembled nothing in the books. I basically shut up about it due to people thinking I was nuts or mistaking it for something else. I can honestly say it was so strange to see that animal or whatever was it and getting so close to it. It looked as though it could have done me in quickly if it had wanted to.

"I am an avid hunter and fisherman to this day but what I saw that day will stick in my mind. My father brought up this incident recently and he thought I should tell this incident. I am thirty-eight now and not too worried about what people think anymore at my age."

Jason wrote a second email affirming that the animal he saw was on all fours, about three-and-one-half feet high, and had dark brown fur that was shaggier on its back. That sounds like it could be a timber wolf, except the animal's tail was quite short, said Jason—only between six inches and one foot long.

"It looked similar to a dog, maybe German shepherd but not quite," he added. "The one thing that sticks in my mind was the eyes. They were black and the stare it gave me was piercing. This animal was like nothing I have ever seen in Wisconsin. I do hunt coyotes and I am a dog owner so I know my canines…. I cannot explain what it was I saw that day. It was no coyote or domestic dog. I am a very responsible person with a good job."

Deer-sized Canine

Another Pleasant Prairie creature showed up in June, 2008, on a narrow, wooded lane called Bain Station Road. Two men were driving east on that road on a clear night between 11:00 p.m. and midnight, one of them wrote, when an animal the size of a deer—but not a deer—ran in front of the headlights. It had very dark, shaggy fur, a canine form, and the men estimated its weight at several hundred pounds.

"We weren't under the influence of anything, and we've never seen anything else considered unusual, nor do we even believe in things such as aliens or UFOs, so this is kind of strange and weird for us to be thinking we saw the beast."

Of course, since the creature was only observed on four feet, it may well have been a large breed of loose dog, perhaps a Russian wolfhound. But it does help shore up the idea that something big and canine roams the woods of Pleasant Prairie.

Beast of Bristol

A huge quadruped was also sighted only ten miles to the west of Pleasant Prairie near Bristol, another Kenosha County town, in April, 2007, on Hwy K (which runs east-west between Paddock Lake and Kenosha through some rural farm areas) at about 1:30 a.m. The three witnesses described it to me as "very large, like bigger than any man." It ran faster as the car approached it, all the while staring with "red, glowing eyes," its head turned toward the vehicle until it disappeared into the woods.

"It still sends chills through all of us," the witness named Kyle wrote, "and we had no idea of a beast so we started researching and found you...."

And finally, a bit farther north between Racine and Milwaukee a man saw something very simi-  lar to the sighting by Lori Endrizzi described in *The Beast of Bray Road*. It was upon Lori's description that I based my "kneeling roadkill" sketch created for the original newspaper story.

The witness, Ted, said that this newer event occurred in 2006 at around 2:00 a.m. as he was driving.

"I saw a large, mangy-looking wolfish creature, with very broad shoulders and a large head. It seemed to be eating road kill. As I drove close to it, it looked up at me, its meal still in its mouth and it was just very weird.

"As I got even with it, it almost looked like it was kneeling like a man on his knees with his lower legs behind him. It all happened so fast but it really creeped me out and I'm not easily scared. It was about man-size, if it was a dog it would have been over 150 pounds. It was a gray-black and scraggly, almost like it was missing patches of hair. I definitely saw pointed ears. The face had grayish fur but it wasn't long like a wolf, it was flatter. Its eyes were piercing and the look it gave sent a chill down my spine.

"Another thing I thought was so strange was it was like forty to eighty yards up an overpass where it couldn't just jump off into the woods. I went and spent a couple hours at the casino but I couldn't wait to come home and tell my wife."

Several years later, Ted mentioned the encounter to some friends and one of them told Ted that he should contact me. Ted said he had no idea my books existed or that the creature had been portrayed on TV shows.

That kneeling posture, I must add, if it is truly kneeling the way a human does, is something that should not be possible for a canine since its "knees" are much higher on its legs than a human's and do not bend in quite the same way. Dogs may crouch or sit on their haunches, but that is a very different action than kneeling. I have no logical way to explain Ted's or Lori's observations.

Milton's "It"

The following email arrived in January, 2008. The events described occurred in Rock County, which adjoins the Illinois border and is the same county where several teens saw three upright canines drinking with their hands from a creek in a large nature preserve west of Janesville. It is also only a short distance from the Lima Marsh area where two other bipedal creature sightings (one with definite Bigfoot characteristics) have been sighted in the past decade:

"I am writing anonymously for many reasons but after seeing the special on the History Channel tonight, I felt compelled to write. I live on the East Coast now but grew up in Rock County, Wisconsin.

"When I was growing up, we used to go to my aunt's house in Milton for family parties. The house was buried in the woods—surrounded by acres of corn and woodland.

"I was probably around ten or twelve years old and it was close to dusk. My aunt's house was on over three acres of land, some of it cleared but most of it woods. Far from the house there was a clearing—it was a large pond with marshes. We had a large family and all the children would play outside and run around. On this particular day, we were playing hide and go seek. I always won because I would find the best hiding places and would stay out the longest.

"It was starting to get dark and I was hiding near the marshes. I saw a couple of my cousins get 'caught' and continued to hide. When everyone was gone, I stood up and saw something odd by the pond —its head looked like a large dog or wolf but it definitely had bipedal movements. "I thought I was seeing things but it scared me so much I ran toward the house, which was pretty far away. I ran into one of my cousins and started screaming that I saw something. For fear of being made fun of, I never told anyone. I told one cousin a few years later but have not told anyone since. The creature did not follow me but we did make eye contact—if I remember correctly it looked as if it was going to the pond to drink."

Having spent a good deal of my own childhood in Milton, this report gave me pause. I played many nighttime games of kick the can in that town! But I don't believe the writer is anyone I know, and I cannot ascertain the date of the incident from the information given. No legends of local monsters come to mind from my school days there, so I don't think Milton residents are primed to expect upright canines in their yards.

What I did notice is that, as usual, the sighting occurred near water and a marshy area.

The Fitchburg Wolf-Quake

A Minnesota college student doing homework while visiting his parents in Fitchburg in September, 2006, was dismayed to hear some prolonged and weird sounds that did not come from his MP3 player.

"I suddenly began hearing loud popping sounds coming from the walls of the house," wrote Matt. "It seemed strange but I didn't think much of it. Then, the frequency of the popping increased while at the same moment, the sound of thousands of birds going crazy erupted from outside in the neighborhood. This was not normal for any time of day, let alone 2:00 a.m."

The twenty-eight-year-old then felt a tremor as the house and ground shook for about five seconds, and he realized both the popping sounds and the frantic birds had been the signals of an impending minor earthquake in the area south of Madison in the southeast corner of Dane County. He tried to settle back into his work, but the weirdness wasn't over.

"Then," he said, "the screaming began. I don't mean little kids playing out in the street. I mean an ear-shattering I-don't-know-what. I was in the basement and could hear it clearly even though it sounded as though it came from across the neighborhood."

Matt went outside where the screaming sound was even louder. It was too loud to be a human, he said, but he wondered if it might be a disturbed child or a person in distress so he began walking down the street toward the source of the sound. As he walked, he remembered uneasily that large animals such as cougars and bears are not unheard of in southern Wisconsin.

A car drove up behind him, and illuminated in the car's headlights he saw a large creature with a distinctly canine head bolt across the road and into an adjacent yard. The screaming had stopped, he said, and the car pulled over to the side of the road. It happened to be a police patrol vehicle, and the policeman asked Matt if he was "the one who called."

Matt replied that he had not called and then asked the policeman if he had come because of the screaming. The officer didn't seem to know about it and drove off to check the neighborhood. As Matt walked home, he heard the scream again from a different direction, but thought better of investigating it this time. "This was more than a howl, a growl, a screech, a yell…whatever. It was human-sounding, but louder than any decibel level a human would be capable of reaching. It's difficult to describe because words do not do it justice. It was freaky."

Matt said that he has had several strange experiences in his life but is not one to jump to supernatural conclusions.

I do wish that he had been able to witness the canine-headed creature making the screaming sound as it crossed the street. Without that visual confirmation, we may only guess that the sound came from the creature he saw. The earthquake casts an eerie shadow over this whole story. Did the animal just happen to be quietly prowling the area when the tremor set off a fear response that resulted in the scream? We may suppose so, but it's impossible to say for sure.

The Whatzit of Watertown

One of my most recent reports as this book goes to press was reported February 2, 2010, the same night a Watertown man having himself an old-fashioned winter cookout just off the Rock River discovered an uninvited guest in his backyard.

The time was around 8:30-8:45 p.m. and the witness was busy grilling steaks on a picnic table in the middle of his yard, despite the threat of snow and a temperature of only 17 degrees Fahrenheit (Wisconsinites will grill in any weather). The man was just retrieving the last piece of meat from the grill after taking the first batch into the house when he saw "someone" moving in the glare of his yard light.

The "someone" appeared to be a very tall person walking briskly around a pine tree only twenty-five feet away. The witness thought it odd that someone would be in his yard at that hour, and he squinted to see the figure. He could make out two "clumsily shuffling legs" and noticed that the figure was walking so close to the tree that branches were moving forward with it and then springing back. The tallest branches moving were higher than the man's head.

"At this point," he wrote, "I started to get a very uneasy feeling (all over queasy feeling, a knot in my stomach; the hair on the back of my neck standing up)." When he later measured the highest branch that he saw moving, it was seven and one-half feet off the ground.

The creature continued on its way out of the yard, trudging fifteen feet to a fence and then cutting alongside the garage where it made considerable noise hopping over piles of scrap metal and leftover building materials. It evidently leaped a three-foot gate and was gone. It did not leave tracks since the snow on the ground at the time had been iced by rain that froze a few days previous to this event.

The man wrote that he worked on the Alaska pipeline for a time and was exposed to many species of bear—and that this creature was nothing like them in its movements and sounds.

Could it have been Bigfoot? The height makes me think it is possible. There have been Bigfoot sightings in Jefferson County, and I can imagine that the aroma of sizzling steaks on a cold February evening would be as likely to bring one hungry meat-eater as another. Lacking footprints or a clear view of the head and body, however, we will have to leave this one in the unidentified BHM (big hairy monster) category and head to another part of the state.

Chapter 21

Central Wisconsin Creatures

Manitowoc County Swamp Thing

The next report, sent by a young woman, is interesting partly because five individuals saw the creature, and partly because the animal they spotted displayed a unique, semi-upright walking posture. The area would be less than an hour's drive to Lake Michigan and fits within the roughly circular area—from Wausau to Green Bay and down to Washington County—that I've identified as a zone where reported creatures often fit the sturdier subtype I call bearwolves.

It is also just west of Maribel Cherney Caves, the area where two young girls reported seeing a more supernatural sort of beast in *Hunting*, and near the burned-out, former resort dubbed "Hotel Hell" in local legend. But neither of those stories would have been well known at the time of this sighting:

"In the summer of 1991 my whole family saw what I now think is the Beast of Bray Road, or some kind of manwolf. I was only eight or nine at the time, and almost thought I was dreaming at first, except everyone else saw it, too. It wasn't a deer or a bear. We never knew what it was, so we called it Swamp Thing, as we saw it in a swampy, marshy area. About a year ago I saw a preview in the beginning of a TV show (I don't know what show) about a Wisconsin werewolf, so I had to watch. It never even occurred to me that it might be the same thing we saw! Of course, I then had to look it up online, and read *The Beast of Bray Road* and *Hunting the American Werewolf* books, too."

The writer's family was caught in a rainstorm that day, as they drove near a series of marshes between Greenleaf and Wayside in a 1989 Camry sedan.

"My dad was driving, my mom was in the front passenger seat, I was in the middle of the back, with my sister and her boyfriend on either side of me. It was late, probably around 11:00 p.m. We were going west on Hwy Z, just past the stop sign where it crosses PP, so I think we were right by the Manitowoc and Brown county border. At that time there were no houses close by, but within the last ten years or so a house was built fairly close to where we saw Swamp Thing. It is kind of a low, swampy area. We have always kept watch for it in that area since we saw it.

"When I first saw it, I thought I was dreaming, until I realized that the car was slowing down and everyone else was seeing it, too. I think someone said something like, 'What IS that?!?' I don't think I was sleeping and woke up, I think I just wasn't expecting it and couldn't believe what I saw. I saw something like a huge dog, with big, upright ears, from the shoulders up with a lot of shaggy, dark fur. The fur seemed especially thick on the back of its neck. The eyes were looking at us and they were yellow. I was only about nine at the time, so for me to see it over the dash, it would have had to be huge.

"I wasn't scared, just curious (I think I was too young, I thought the car could protect us). I remember wanting to stop, telling my dad to stop, maybe turn around and check it out again. It's strange, because when I was little, the only monster I was scared of was the werewolf, I had a recurring nightmare about one chasing me. I never even placed (this creature) in that category when I saw it. When we drove past the spot where it ran into the ditch, I don't remember actually seeing it watching us from the ditch, maybe just the eyes, but I knew it was there.

"My dad said the face looked kind of like a German shepherd, long, with greenish-yellow eyes. It was dark colored. It ran from left to right across the road in front of the car, in a stooped over position, to the ditch. The front arms were for balance, somewhat like a monkey. It stopped in the ditch and watched us go past in a challenging manner. [My dad] said it was very weird and stupid looking. He commented that every time he has gone down that stretch of road he gets a funny feeling and doesn't want to hang around. I got the creeps when he described it in detail, because he never read your books, and his description was very much like some of the others in your books.

"My mom just couldn't believe what she saw, and when I asked her, she just said it was weird and strange. When I asked for a better description, she said it was like a huge, powerful thing, almost more human than wolf. Like it could do anything it wanted. My family has discussed it, and we agreed even at the time, and now, that it couldn't be a human in a costume. It was too big, too real, and what would a person be doing in a storm on a highway at night. There was a chance of no cars going by at all. We drove through that area all the time at all hours, and it was always really dead at night and in the early morning. Sometimes we wouldn't encounter any other traffic.

"My sister, about seventeen at the time, didn't really see it when it was in the road, in the headlights. She watched it as it was 'peeking at us' from on the side of the road, in the ditch. She said it was like a huge dog, bigger than a human man, with black-gray shaggy fur, a long snout and a wolfish appearance. She described the eyes as red and glowing, and it stood on two bent-backward dog legs. She said that even in the ditch, it had to bend down to look in at us. She definitely didn't want to stop, because it looked big enough to disable the car if it so chose. She said whenever she had to drive through there alone or at night after we saw it, she would be kind of freaked out.

"She said she talked about it with her boyfriend at the time, who was also in the car. He had the same description as her, and they agreed that it was scary but cool.

"When we were talking about it, I made the offhand comment that I had my one chance to see a monster, and I didn't get a good enough look at it to really clearly remember it in detail. My sister said that I wouldn't want to. The more I think about it, I agree. Thanks for hearing me out and writing the Beast books, because for years we thought we were the only people who had seen this thing. Even if we don't know what it is, at least we know it has shown itself to others."

My first question was about the evident discrepancy in eye color, since the sister reported the eyes as red while the others saw the more usual green-yellow color that is the normal eyeshine of canines caught in the headlights. She wasn't sure why her sister saw or remembered the color as red, but speculated that she might have seen them at a different angle in the ditch, where the lights did not shine directly at the creature. That may be possible, or it may be that after twenty years, the sister might have incorporated the typical movie monster eye color, red, into her memories of the actual creature. Other than that, this family seemed very united in their belief that this was one unusual canine.

Walk Like a Hyena

The region about forty miles west of Green Bay is swathed with huge wildlife areas and wetlands. Late one night in November, 2007, a fifty-one-year-old woman and her sixteen-year-old daughter were driving home toward Clintonville on State Route 156 when something really strange shuffled slowly onto the road in front of their Dodge Caravan's headlights.

A partial moon helped reveal something that reminded them of a giant hyena with long "arms" in front and shorter hind legs that brought its rear closer to the ground. Even on all fours, it stood as tall as a man. Its front limbs appeared human-like but larger, and the creature appeared to be walking on the "knuckles" or fronts of its front paws.

The woman stopped her car to let the creature continue crossing and was able to get a very good look at it. She estimated its weight at 250 pounds, minimum, and it had short, wiry dark brown-and-gray fur. She described its head as "shaped similar to that of a wolf, but the snout seemed much wider and the head was larger and covered with shaggy fur." No teeth were visible but both women noticed long, thick black claws on the closest front paw. Its eyes reflected yellow. Its rear end was also shaggy and they couldn't tell if it had a tail. The women later identified the animal as similar to my indigenous dogman sketch on my website after another relative told them about it.

The oddest thing about this sighting in my opinion, however, is the creature's posture and odd position of the front paws when walking. Apes walk on their knuckles but they don't have claws or "wolf-shaped" heads. Baboons (Old World monkeys) have short muzzles but they have nearly bare rumps and very visible tails, with the largest males weighing only about eighty pounds—far short of this creature's estimated 250 pounds.

It seems to me, though, that the posture may have been an extreme example of the "hunched over" position described by so many other witnesses. The animal may also have injured its front limbs, an explanation that would help explain its slowness as it made its way to the brush on the other side.

This wasn't the first strange thing this woman had seen; she saw a UFO as a child and believes she has experienced ghostly "activity" in her home, but this is fairly common and the teenager claimed no supernatural events in her life. And large, unidentifiable canid sightings were absent from both women's previous histories.

The Threat in Theresa

Theresa is a historic little town that I drive through whenever I'm headed to the Fox River Valley area of Wisconsin. Set at the intersection of State Routes 67 and 175 about eight miles east of the Horicon Marsh, it had previously attracted my attention for a mention I'd found of "giant," ancient Native American remains discovered there in a burial mound. A Catholic church was said to have been built over the mound.

But in November, 2006, Theresa moved up a notch on my personal interest graph when I received an email from Josh—a young man in the U.S. military who recounted an experience he had in 1992 when he was eight years old.

Josh lived on a small farm two miles south of town on Allen Road, and he remembers it was early afternoon sometime in spring of that year when he was riding his bicycle around the farmyard between the garage and the barn. This route led him past a fenced section of woods that bordered a marsh. He noticed, as he rode, that the farm animals had all disappeared from view and thought that was odd.

"I looked down the hill by the woods," he wrote, "and saw something gray and tall walking. It was very large and hairy, its fur was a dirty gray color. I looked at some of the sketches on your (web) page, and it was pretty close. I didn't get a real good look at the face since it was about 250 meters away. It did walk past this antique corn planter which was five feet tall so I'm guessing (the creature) was six to seven feet tall. It walked upright but not straight. It leaned over a little from the waist. The head was rather large, too. It walked very fast and I got out of there as quick as I could. I wouldn't go back there or even near the barn for a very long time alone. That was the only time I saw the 'thing.' I told my parents and they said I was making it up." Josh's parents never forgot his story, however, and when they saw an article about my books, they sent it to him and he contacted me.

Rubicon Bearwolf

Less than twenty miles south of Theresa, between the Rubicon River and Butler Creek, is the modest berg of Rubicon. It lies far enough east of State Route 67 that it is dangerously close to the cluster of Holy Hill bearwolf sightings, but since in my own mind I usually lump it with Theresa and the route to Fond du Lac, I'll leave this brief, second-hand account in this chapter.

A Rubicon woman wrote me in 2007 that her brother-in-law's friend witnessed something strange after taking his dogs outside to do their late night duties on March 7 of that year. He had gone back into the house to wait for them when he heard them start to bark. Hustling back outside, he spotted an animal in a nearby field. This "animal" was walking upright, he said, shifting its weight from side to side on its hind legs. He could see it very clearly, he told her. It had the head of a wolf and a "broader" body with dark fur. It disappeared into the brush, and he and his dogs went back in the house.

It is possible that this was a bear, although the extended two-legged walking makes that unlikely. The wolf-like head and broad body make it sound very like a bearwolf. Peg it as another unknown biped.

The Poynette Snarler

A man from Juneau named Pat certainly piqued my interest in April, 2009 when he wrote me that he had seen a "wolf/canine from Hell" near Poynette. It had happened four or five years earlier, he said, putting the date at 2004 or 2005. And he did remember the exact time and place: three a.m. on State Route 22 just north of the MacKenzie Environmental Education Unit in the northeastern corner of Dane County.

As he passed a house near a field of tall grass that night on his way home from work, he saw an animal crouched at the edge of the field with some kind of carcass between its feet. Its ears were laid back, its teeth were bared and it appeared to be snarling at Pat and his truck as he slowed for a better look.

"What was so strange was the size and color," he said. "It was as tall as the grass, about two feet, even though it was in a crouched, ready-to-spring position and (it was) as black as a black lab. Its hair was standing up and it looked pissed. I looked at it as I went by and thought, 'What the heck was that?' I've seen wolves, dogs, coyotes and bears. This was best described as a 'canine from Hell.' A rabid animal would not be eating road kill."

Pat whipped his truck around and returned to the spot but the creature was gone, leaving only an obviously matted area of grass. But he was still convinced of what he had seen. "I got a good look at it as I went by," he said. "I had my bright lights on and saw the reflection of eyes first, then looked right at it and it was looking right at me. I don't recall what color the eyes were. This happened about five years ago but when one sees things like that one does not forget."

It sounds to me like whatever Pat saw was acting defensively over its supper. It could well have been a very large, black wolf—it's hard to positively identify anything sitting in crouched position—or perhaps a feral dog of some type. The bottom line is that it impressed a man familiar with state wildlife as being something unknown, and although the beast did not stand up, it fit the other usual characteristics—size, ferocity, dark fur, canine appearance and accessorized with road kill—very well, indeed.

Also, it tallies well with another sighting just a few miles to the south near Arlington only a year or so earlier in 2003, when a woman and her mother both saw a "hunched over" canine running across the road on its hind legs. (See *Hunting the American Werewolf*.)

Chapter 22

Northwoods Nasties

Wisconsin's northern environs can be thought of as the bulbous part of the state's "light bulb" shape. That encompasses a lot of territory but might include everything north of a line drawn from La Crosse to Green Bay. Many will quibble over the exact boundaries of "up north," but since the land begins to change and the population starts to thin above that artificial line, it will do for the purposes of this book.

Logically, the majority of Wisconsin cryptid reports should come from this region of vast forests, numerous waterways and stretches of Great Lakes shoreline, but this is not so. It may be that more manwolves (and other things) do find shelter and game here, but there are fewer people in the area to see and report them. The same scenario holds true between Michigan's Upper and Lower Peninsulas: massive wilderness, lower population, fewer reports.

This doesn't mean that northern manwolf encounters do not occur. And sometimes they are all the more intense simply because they are more likely to be out in the wild, far from other humans who might at least hear the screams...

Tomahawk Terror

The terror started in late August, 2008, for a family living near a wooded area outside of Tomahawk in Lincoln County. A teenaged son was walking to the family's mailbox when he saw something crossing the road about 100 feet away. He watched, incredulous, as it continued on two legs into the woods on the other side. He described it as dark or black in color, man-sized, and having a very broad chest that narrowed at the hips. The head appeared canid, with a longer snout than a bear's. Since he was so close to the creature and had very good light, the teen felt he was able to see it very well. And he saw enough to know better than to follow it into the woods.

Little did he know that was only the beginning of a long-time "relationship" that the family came to dread. First, his mother heard something smash into the steel siding on their house one night, hard enough that the whole ranch house shook. When she investigated the next day, it was strongly dented eight feet off the ground and there was also a big scratch. The deep dent and scratch both seemed too large for some errant night bird to have made.

The teen's younger brother began to hear something walking on what sounded like two feet, crunching the gravel on the driveway beneath his window, where the footsteps would stop and stand before slowly walking away again. The boys' mother told me it got so bad that her younger son refused to sleep in his own room and started sacking out on the living room sofa instead.

The mother also supplied a supporting incident. A neighbor told her he had seen the same wolf-like, bipedal creature ten years earlier. The man had a junkyard and was working in it one warm fall evening when he looked up and saw the creature staring at him from the edge of the woods only twenty yards away. He dropped his work and ran for the house. To his horror, the creature ran after him but "veered away" as the man neared his house.

She also told me that she had an unsettling feeling of being watched whenever she was outside in her garden. And she mentioned that there have been numerous sightings of UFOs, some as low as treetop level and one made by the Lincoln County Sheriff in 1981, along the Wisconsin River near where these creature sightings took place. Her own mother and sister saw a large triangle UFO while canoeing several years earlier.

The ongoing nature of this case reminds me very much of the one in Akron, Ohio. In both circumstances, the creature seems to notice a young male and then begins to stalk the residence while paying special attention to windows. In Ohio, the creature stole a squawking rooster as if trying to attract attention and in this case, it (presumably) asserted itself by bashing in and scratching the siding. Although I hate to read too much into this, both actions strike me as tactics designed to draw someone out of the house. And I don't like the sound of that at all.

The proximity of UFO sightings brings to mind another case south of Wausau, which is only about thirty-five miles to the south.

The Wausau Whatzit

While some creature sightings last only seconds, cases like the Tomahawk incident and the one I am about to explore can involve a chain of incidents and puzzling, additional phenomena.

I received an email in October, 2006, from a man who recounted "numerous incidents by Lake Du Bay, in Mosinee woods, south of Wausau." The events began in the late 1980s, when he was 13, and continued into the early 1990s. It began with the appearance of unidentified lights near the Little Eau Pleine River, part of a large chain of waterways near the George W. Meade Wildlife Area.

Witness sketch of the Wausau Whatzit

He and his friends were sitting around a campfire in his parents' hay field in the winter one night about eight o'clock, eating pizza and pelting one another with snowballs. Suddenly a powerful beam of light appeared in the trees edging the field and moved toward the young teens. The light moved in a circle around them twice over the space of about twenty seconds and terrified the group because they could not discover any source for it.

After the light disappeared, they shrugged it off as a fluke. But other lights spooked them three years later when they were sixteen, at the Little Eau Pleine River next to the writer's farm. He and his friend Ryan were out sneaking a smoke behind their corn crib that overlooked the river when they noticed small globes of light moving in a slow, constant direction and height about twenty-five feet over the creek toward Lake DuBay. There were three identical lights, evenly spaced. He and Ryan returned often after that and saw the same phenomenon on several other nights.

He also observed a large, white, glowing oval object floating toward Lake DuBay while looking out his living room window one night. He checked the time, 1:56 a.m., and then was surprised to see it come floating back just six minutes later. It began to ascend and then stopped briefly after rising a few hundred feet, rose again, stopped, then shot off toward the creek leaving a bright streak tailing behind it.

"Now looking back and seeing what I saw later," he wrote, "I think it was picking something up."

He continued camping on his parents' land with his friends, and they began to experience the strange beam illuminating their campsite from time to time. And then they started to notice a "triangular" head popping out of the nearby cornfield, followed by rustling sounds. That ended the camping.

Not long after, one of his friends was driving past the hill where the last incident had occurred when something large slammed into the side of his Chevy S-10 pickup. It followed him home and tore gardening tools off the outside of his family's shed as he parked his truck, but never showed itself.

Another friend, Jason, was crossing a bridge over the Little Eau Pleine not far from the camp area when he spotted a canine-like creature hunched over in the ditch. As his headlights lit up the roadside, the creature rose to its hind legs and began to run upright. He estimated its height at over six feet and said it was a grayish tan color. After it crossed the road it dropped to all fours and continued toward the river.

A week after that, the writer wanted to test the radio in his new '82 Skylark, so he and Jason drove out to the camping hill where they could crank up the volume. After testing the sound to their satisfaction, they drove off, making a U-turn on the intersection of County Road DB and Sunset. But as the Skylark's lights swung around, the two young men were shocked to see the same creature standing in a hunched posture in the center of the road. It stared at them with large yellow eyes set beneath pointed ears from only fifteen feet away.

Except for canid legs, the body was human-like, the writer said, with no fur and grayish tan, oily skin. It was so thin that its ribs were visible, and it had no tail.

The creature turned and dashed away on its hind legs at an incredible speed and was not seen again.

What to make of the unidentifiable lights that preceded the appearance of the furless, upright canine? Some researchers have long noted associations between odd lights, UFOs and other creatures such as Bigfoot. I have always pointed out that these associations can only be considered circumstantial unless there is some direct link between the two. Still, even though the writer never observed the creature in or interacting with the light beams or the glowing oval, it does seem odd that both things would occur in the same isolated area within a certain time frame and in relation to this one group of young men.

The behavior of both the lights and the creature suggests some type of purposeful observation—or harassment—of the teens. Why and by whom is anyone's guess.

The Range of Mange

One more topic needs a brief look here, and that is the parasitic scourge of mammals known as Sarcoptic mange, a disease caused by the *Sarcoptes scabiei* mite. A major symptom is severe fur fall-out. The bare patches, which look oily just as the witness observed, can radically alter an animal's appearance; it is hard to overestimate the impact the loss of thick fur may have on any creature's recognizability.

Over the past few years, a variety of creatures—always ultimately identified by zoologists as mundane animals such as coyotes or foxes with mange—have shown up in photos on cryptozoology sites labeled as *chupacabras* or "monsters" although the beasts possess neither unusual size nor unknown characteristics other than disfigurement due to decomposition. Could the grayish-tan creature of the Little Eau Pleine River have been a large wolf, dog or bear with a bad case of mange? It would certainly explain the animal's naked look—but not its size or its habit of running upright. Perhaps manwolves can get mange, too.

Two decades later, another mangy, upright animal showed up a little to the north.

Mangy Mutt of Black River Falls

The Black River runs through it, the Black River State Forest lies to its east, Cranberry Flowage and Fort McCoy Military Reservation flank its south, and forested, sparsely populated areas blanket the land to its west and north. It should come as no surprise then that Black River Falls in Jackson County should be the site of a rather weird creature report that occurred in 2004.

A woman named Chris and her boyfriend were walking home one fall night in a well-lit area of the city when a wolf-like creature dashed around a corner toward them on four feet. When it saw the couple, it stopped and stood up in a hunched position only fifty to seventy-five feet away for a brief stare-down. In that position it appeared to be about five and one-half feet tall.

The creature was panting from its hard run, said Chris, and they could see a mouthful of long teeth inside a muzzle about the length of an Afghan hound's. Its feet and legs were canine and it ran on its toe pads, with hind limbs that were noticeably more muscular than the front limbs. The front paws had either elongated "fingers" or long claws. The body also appeared very muscular, and it was covered with patchy fur as if suffering from a case of mange. "It had a fat torso and longer limbs that were not proportioned right," she said. She and her boyfriend went straight home and drew the accompanying sketch of it after it ran off into the night across someone's lawn.

Chris said they did not fear the creature, even though it made no noise while running and that fact struck them as unnatural. Indeed, they felt the creature feared them. She said others around town also saw it, and she believes "100 percent that this 'thing' exists."

"I know what I saw and I'm not insane," said Chris.

This is how it stood when it looked at us, but its shoulder and upper body, was facing in a more foward direction and it had one front foot/hand down as it rounded the corner.

Chris

Witness sketch by Chris

Bearded Ladysmith Creature

While I have been selecting only the more striking reports of strictly quadruped creatures, this incident from Ladysmith in 2002 hit me as so beyond the pale that it deserved inclusion.

A Racine man born in Ladysmith returned to his home town that October for bow hunting. At the time of his encounter he was driving with his uncle along a little road by the Hubbard town hall, which is located on County Hwy J. The Flambeau River flows along next to the county road, which matches the river's curves.

The man told me in a phone interview that their headlights shone into a field to reveal "it" standing there staring at them from forty to fifty yards away.

"It was the size of a horse," he said, "real stocky and muscular. I can still see it plain as day. Its eyes reflected red. Its head came down in a snout that had a point, the muzzle was more like a lab than a German shepherd. I could not see the ears. It was very hairy. Matted hair covered the head and body. It had a beard that wasn't real long, it was almost like a goat's. The hair there was four to five inches long."

"It kind of shocked me," he continued. "It seemed very solid. I felt it was just challenging us like a dog will stare at you. It wasn't moving. After maybe three minutes it turned and walked real slow on all fours and disappeared into the woods. It didn't move like any other kind of animal. It had a presence. I almost had a feeling like it was evil or something."

"We were silent at first and then we just looked at each other."

The creature may have left some evidence. The man's uncle has a cabin nearby and found two odd footprints near it. He said they were seventeen inches long and eight inches wide, barefoot and human-like. That sounds like Bigfoot, except the big toe was "split" and there were claw marks in front of each toe point. The man's uncle and aunt took photos and promised photos if they turned out well, but I never received them. I must say I have never seen nor heard of any others matching that description.

The Eau Claire Twilight Zone

Eau Claire is known as a college town with its bustling University of Wisconsin campus, but the 65,000-plus-population city first soared with the state's early lumbering industry, like so many other northern Wisconsin communities. Rumors say it harbors the usual ghosts of old loggers and lumber barons left skulking in such towns, but no other apparent reason exists to explain the extreme oddity of its creature sightings.

Two people have reported incidents in Eau Claire. Both include strange elements, so I advise strapping yourself firmly into your Barca-lounger before proceeding; you're in for a harrowing read.

Author interpretation of creature seen by two different men in Eau Claire

Sneaking Creature

For about a decade, Eau Claire area residents have had the opportunity to attend an annual paranormal conference hosted by Unexplained Research, the publisher of this book. I have been a speaker at that conference more than once, and at one of the events, I showed a sketch I had made of a black-furred "wolfman" that appeared to an Eau Claire man in his Cameron Street apartment (See *Hunting the American Werewolf*).

A man who had attended the conference wrote later that he had seen something that looked almost exactly like my drawing in his Eau Claire backyard, about a mile from Cameron Street, in July, 2008. He wrote:

"The picture in your presentation brought a chill in me. The picture was almost identical to something I saw three months ago. The only thing different is it was brown and the muzzle wasn't as protruded."

The man had been mowing his lawn near dusk, he said, and suddenly had the feeling he was being watched. He looked up to see if it was a friend that lived nearby, perhaps waiting for him to shut off the mower for a chat, but it was not.

"Between my truck and the garage was that *thing* in the drawing, kinda sneaking. The only way I could describe the movement is how you see a ninja moving in the movies." He estimated it stood about six feet tall, and he felt that it wanted him to see it.

The writer said he stared in disbelief, and then the creature looked directly at him and instantly disappeared. "The thing looked a little blurry around the edges," he said, "almost like a picture not totally in focus, but the further center of the body looked more solid."

He said that he tried to convince himself that it was just some sort of shadow, but when he saw my drawing he knew instantly that it was what he had seen. And that would be an upright, muscular creature covered in short, dark fur with a dog-like head and pointed ears. The creature did not frighten him, however.

"I seriously had the feeling that this was something that was trying to watch over me, not to harm me, maybe like a 'spirit animal' type relationship if that makes sense?"

The Cameron Street incident occurred five years earlier, in May, 2003, and that "creature" also disappeared as it realized it was observed. Because of the poof factor, however, it may be more accurate to call both of these entities canine apparitions rather than creatures.

It's interesting that two unrelated men in the same city would both see this vanishing, humanoid-canine, making me wonder whether others also saw it. These incidents—and the "visitor" itself—are quite different from the great bulk of manwolf sightings, most of which have no overtly supernatural features. But read on…

Eau Claire Snow Chaser

The following incident was first reported to Terry Fisk of Unexplained Research by a thirty-five-year-old man and his teenaged son. Terry passed it on to me, noting the pair was unaware of my books or that anyone else had ever seen something similar. I interviewed the man, who works in the transportation industry, by phone and will try to summarize my lengthy notes—he and his son had quite an evening...

They were driving home to Mondovi after a concert in Eau Claire in late fall, 2004. In the process of heading through town for State Route 37, they somehow found themselves blocked by a snowdrift and forced down a treacherous dirt lane surrounded by a tunnel of ice-laden trees. To make things worse the engine kept quitting.

They finally got turned back around to Clairemont Avenue, one of the main thoroughfares and then decided to stop for a snack at the Blimpie's on Garfield, right next to the Chippewa River which flows through the center of town. But when they made the turn for the restaurant, they found themselves back on that country road, and the engine again started to die every few minutes.

The son was terrified by this time, but the weirdest events were just beginning. The car went into a slide, and a huge animal—the father described it as something like a big, cartoonish elk so tall that it towered over the Ford Contour sedan—jumped out from the trees. It looked in at the father and son and snorted so hard that steam came from its nostrils and then ran across the road with five other bulky, similar animals behind it. It had very long horns with only a few points, he said.

I must admit that had the son not seen everything too, I might have wondered if the dad was hallucinating. He did finally make it back to another road, and yet as soon as he turned to get onto Hwy 37, he found himself back on the same strange back road for a third time with the engine stopping every 50-100 yards. The son became hysterical. Again they proceeded as best they could, continually forced to restart the engine.

At last they came to a sharp bend in the road. The father checked the rearview mirror as he negotiated the turn and spotted a different kind of creature crossing the road about thirty yards behind him. It was some kind of huge canine on all fours with a swagger in its shoulders. And then the car died again.

The son turned around to see what his dad was looking at, and the creature reared up on its hind legs and took a few steps while upright. It then dropped back to all fours and dashed at the car. The son began to scream. By the time the creature was only ten yards away the dad got the car started again and made it around the curve, and the creature again rose up and followed on its hind legs. Both father and son were screaming now. Within a minute, though, it dropped back to all fours and sauntered into the snowy woods.

"I thought it was a werewolf, and we're not science fiction nerds," said the dad in his interview. "I still don't know what to call it, it was not a bear, a wolf or a dog. The road was white and this thing was black and it was a mammoth of an animal."

They were not able to see its face but the son saw its red tongue hanging from its muzzle as it followed them around the curve.

"We couldn't see its tail but it had a long kind of body and a huge back," said the dad. "I felt it was really after us. It was dumbfounding."

They kept going and within a few minutes were back in civilization and on their way home.

I do need to mention that in the weeks prior to this eerie experience, the man, his wife and son witnessed a giant, black triangular UFO traveling slowly only 300 feet above them as they drove west on US Route 10 from Mondovi to Durand between 9:30 and 10:00 p.m. The exact location was at Zittel Road between Bear Creek and Bear Creek Swamp.

They had first noticed some lights in an adjacent cornfield, and his wife asked him to turn around to see what they were. When he tried to pull back onto the highway, he said, "a darkening happened" as the night sky overhead seemed to cast a deep shadow. That's when they looked up and saw the craft. It was as long as a football field and made no sound, he said, and they watched it continue on its way until it disappeared into the horizon.

A few days later, around the same time they saw the creature, they again saw a strange light on Zittel and the light rushed the car, staying on their bumper as t hey sped off to get away from it. It disappeared when they made their turn.

The father described himself as a rational man who grew up in another state and never experienced anything out of the ordinary before these incidents, nor does he consider himself "open" to such events. Terry Fisk believed him a credible witness.

The parallels to the "Wausau Whatzit" are obvious: observation of oddly-behaving aerial lights followed by sightings of bizarre creatures that seem focused on a particular individual or group. But the family's stunning view of the unknown, triangular black craft brings this whole case foursquare into UFO-land. Even the phenomenon of the car's engine stalling for no apparent reason only on the strange back road is a common feature of UFO reports worldwide.

And still we are left to guess at the implied relationship between these strange insertions into the landscape of Eau Claire. Were the weird elk-thing and the upright canine passengers of the triangle craft? Holographic projections emanating from the UFO or some other source? Portions of a unified trickster spirit matrix? Wildly misidentified human aircraft, deer (or elk) herd and wolf?

The answer you choose, wise reader, depends upon your own belief system, biases, and judgment unless, like me, you conclude there is not enough evidence to render a valid decision one way or the other. I must admit, though, that the idea of a spirit trickster I will discuss further in the last section of the book solves this particular string of events in the tidiest way. If only we possessed the technology to prove it beyond a shadow-creature of doubt.

Chapter 23

Bray Road Revisited

People commonly think that all sightings of upright unknown canines in the world occur solely along the two-mile byway outside of Elkhorn, Wisconsin known as Bray Road. I have purposely saved this chapter for last to show that incidents at this location are only a tiny fragment of total reports nationwide. And yet I am often asked, "What's new on Bray Road?"

The truth is that sightings nosedived for a decade after about 1993-1994, when Bray Road cruising became a popular recreational pastime for legions of hopeful werewolf seekers. If some sort of indigenous, biped-adapted wolf had lived there, it would have been driven out by this invasion of crowds in camo and the constant glare of headlights. For those who believe the Beast is non-corporeal, well, supernatural entities also seem to function best in more desolate locations. It's no wonder the canine media star moved to darker highways.

And yet, more sightings have come to my attention—some old and some new. I'm including sightings within about a thirty-mile radius of Bray Road since that would be a normal prowling range for any large predator. I'll start with one of the most recent—and most unusual.

Baby Beast

State Route 50 is a busy highway that runs between Geneva Lake and Lake Como on its way from Delavan into the City of Lake Geneva.

The spot where it intersects Schofield Road at the El Dorado subdivision is only about eight miles south of Bray Road, and the land between is mostly farms, woods, and lake neighborhoods.

This is where a forty-three-year-old man and his fifteen-year-old daughter saw something cross the highway at about 9:00 p.m. the night of Tuesday, January 26, 2010. The sky was overcast, the man wrote me, but visibility was good as the creature popped out of the ditch on the south side of the highway near Wood Elementary School and ran north across the road illuminated by their headlights.

It ran on its hind legs. And it was only three to four feet tall. It was covered in long, black or dark brown fur and had a dog-like tail and pointed ears—definitely canine. He described its walk as a fast lope. It ran straight for a woodlot where the pair lost sight of it, on two legs all the way.

The family lives in that neighborhood and the man said they had been hearing strange vocalizations and sounds before the sighting.

Reports of creatures of this size, roughly half the height cited in most cases, are rare. The other example that comes to mind is the "half-pint" seen by two bicyclers on the Larsen Trail west of Oshkosh in 1990. Might these have been baby beasts? It stands to reason that if man-wolves are flesh-and-blood creatures they must have young ones.

Or perhaps—although the fur color doesn't fit—we are looking at sightings of a were-coyote.

Corn Runner

UW-Whitewater student Haley Smith of Delavan was a frequent visitor to Bray Road in the fall of 2006 because she was dating a young man who lived there. The eighteen-year-old was just backing out of his driveway one evening at dusk, turning her car at a forty-five degree angle to face the adjacent cornfield, when she saw a tall, brown-furred figure running upright through the cornstalks.

"He was so tall his head was above the fully grown corn," she said. That would put the creature at six to seven feet tall. His head appeared very large, she noted.

When the creature saw her headlights it dropped to all fours and she could no longer see it, but she was so shaken that she backed behind some trees by the driveway and could not drive herself home.

Mobile Home Monster

One end of Bray Road ends up on the edge of Elkhorn on Geneva Street as it turns into Township Route NN, a road that leads to the hospital, county courthouse and sheriff's department. Near that intersection is Elkhorn High School and, a little closer to town but separated by a strip mall, a mobile home park.

A man wrote me in January, 2008, that in the previous month (December, 2007) he was visiting friends at their mobile home when he spotted something near the high school. I interviewed him about the events of that day by phone.

It was slightly foggy and near dusk as he drove his truck out of the park entrance onto Geneva Street, but he noticed at once that something very large and dark was walking fast and upright, heading for Bray Road. The man followed in his truck, turning right onto Geneva Street and then making the left onto Bray. He drove the road slowly but didn't see the creature, so he turned around and came back the same way, examining every field. Finally, after about twenty minutes, he looked toward a wooded area and saw the creature heading for it, walking through a low field.

"I could see it from the stomach up," he said. "It was between seven and eight feet tall. That second time I could see it was covered in hair, it was not someone in a big costume. The legs appeared bent backward and it was lunging forward, hunched over at the neck."

It disappeared into the woods on two legs.

The man told his friends at the mobile home park what he had seen, and they shared the troubling information that their cat was missing. Astute readers will remember that upright canines have been caught in the act of pet-napping in other states.

Beast in Wolf's Clothing?

One man wrote me that he had lived in a log cabin on Bray Road in the 1980s, before there was any publicity, and that he had seen the beast about 6:00 a.m. one sunny morning on his way to work. It was leaping through a field like a deer, he said, and as he slowed down for a better look, the animal ran in front of his car only ten feet away.

"Do you know what it was?" he wrote. "It was a VERY LARGE GREY WOLF (emphasis writer's). Not common in the area, but that's without question what it was."

The only problem is that since wolves in the wild seldom live more than ten years, this was not likely to have been the same creature sighted as late as 2007.

Other than that, I can certainly believe the writer. Someone else from Bray Road has told me the same thing—that the beast is a garden variety grey wolf. There are without doubt grey wolves in Wisconsin, and it is always wise to obey Occam's Razor and wade around in the simple, mundane explanations before diving into the deep, paranormal end. After all, the creatures are usually described as wolf-like. Their eyes are yellow like those of wolves, and even the challenging stare and menacing "sneer" are standard behaviors from a wolf in a threatening posture. But we still don't know why so many witnesses have seen them

Bray Road where it ends at State Hwy 11 between Elkhorn and Burlington

standing and running on two feet, sometimes alternating with all fours. That just is not standard behavior, and I cannot find any observations from wolf specialists to support it.

I have, however, received several interesting reports of large wolf-like creatures on all fours in this area. Since this is Bray Road, the perceived epicenter of sightings, and since it is possible that these particular canids chose not to reveal their two-footed locomotion skills at the time they were spotted, I'll summarize them for the record. They do at the very least support the contention that very large, wolf-like creatures roam this area:

- March, 2004: Three UW-Whitewater students were driving a 1997 Cavalier east along State Route 50 on their way to O'Hare Airport in Chicago in the early evening, when something ran in front of the car. The driver and writer, Jeff, hit the brakes and was amazed when it appeared that he hadn't hit the large creature. One of his friends also saw it and they agreed it was too tall to be even a very large dog, that it had a thick, gray coat and that it moved incredibly fast. This would have been within twenty to thirty miles of Bray Road, and even closer to another series of sightings near Powers Lake in 2006 (see below).

- November 19, 2007: A man who worked at the Walworth County complex was driving on NN at 5:15 p.m. and saw a large canine sitting on the side of the road with its head level to that of the man's, who was seated in an SUV. He estimated it as six feet tall while seated. He described it as dark-furred, not a bear, too big to be a dog, with light eyes and bright eyeshine. It had a muzzle and legs more muscular than a dog's.

- August 21, 2007: A woman was traveling with her mother and two daughters on Bowers Road (runs parallel with Bray) just after 8:00 p.m. when near the intersection with Loveland they spied an animal running across the road on all fours. It ran in a gallop so smooth it appeared to almost float, was black-furred and the size of a month-old calf and exhibited yellow eyeshine. Its head, she said, was like a Great Dane's with pointed ears and a long snout and it was thick-chested. Her mother also saw it.

- April 7, 2008: A woman who describes herself as a scientist, hunter and outdoorswoman saw a large, tailless creature that was not a dog or bear on Antique Road in Eagle, about fifteen miles north of Bray

Road. She watched from her car as the dark grey-black animal approached a steep bank on the other side of the road and pulled itself up mainly using its forelimbs. She estimated less than half its weight was on its hind legs, and she was impressed by its air of confidence and ease of movement as it negotiated the bank. A trained biologist, she was so baffled that she told a colleague about it the next day, and he recommended she contact me. She was not tired or drunk, she said, and was terrified because she didn't know what "it" was.

- January 26, 1992: A man was driving on NN to visit his wife and newborn son at Lakeland Hospital when a very large, gray creature appeared in the headlights of his vehicle on the driver's side. The creature began to run alongside his car, keeping pace with it and sometimes even outracing it momentarily to appear in the headlights again. This continued for about a mile at a speed of about fifty-five miles per hour. It only broke off after the man, beginning to panic, sped up to sixty-five miles per hour. He only had a quick glimpse of the creature's face from the side, but it had a huge chest, heavily muscled legs, and was larger than an Irish wolfhound.

Lair of the Lakes

In the summer of 1991, a year before the story of the Beast broke, a family driving on State Route 67 heading north to Lauderdale Lakes included a thirteen-year-old boy who spotted a strange creature near the White Horse restaurant (which has since burned down). He wrote me fifteen years later after finding my website, still haunted by the memory.

"I saw it as we were driving at night," he wrote. "It looked as if it were eating something about twenty feet off the road. As we drove by it looked up and it was not human—very hairy, a long snout, and large." He also noticed pointed, hairy ears. The creature rose to its hind legs and stood in a hunched position as the car continued past it.

"I swear it looked me in the eyes and I still have nightmares about it."

He told his parents, but predictably, they did not believe him.

The site where this occurred is about eight miles north of Elkhorn and very close to Lake Wandawega as well as Lauderdale, at the edge of the southern unit of the Kettle Moraine State Forest. The Lauderdale Lakes area was part of a well-worn Amerindian trail and contained many ancient burial mounds when settlers arrived.

Biped of The Knobs

A large biped was also spotted in the early 90s—about eight miles southeast of Bray Road near Lyons on Knob Road in the area known locally as "The Knobs." It's only two miles west of Bohner's Lake and a system of ponds and creeks.

The person who wrote grew up in that area and was a friend of the actual witness, so I did not get a first-hand report. The witness saw the large, hairy creature standing on the side of the road as he drove by on a winter morning, but the writer did not include enough of a description to know that it was canine. The most interesting part of this story is that the creature appeared aware that it was being observed and tried to hide behind a tree.

The writer said his friend has mentioned the incident many times over the years, and that he had complete faith in the friend's integrity. The fact that the creature was trying to get out of sight is consistent with most other sightings of manwolves.

Commuter Creature

One of the most compelling cases in the area happened from February to April, 2008, twelve to fifteen miles southeast of Bray Road near Powers Lake. The witness had a very high security clearance as an airport employee and therefore did not want anything disclosed about his identity. In fact, his sister contacted me first and then I interviewed the witness, whom I will call Rob, by phone.

His sister explained how out of character these experiences were for Rob. "This is the last thing he would ever talk about," she said. "He would never, ever think of something like this; he doesn't believe in this kind of stuff."

Disbelief notwithstanding, Rob had seen a strange canine three times on a stretch of road he drove every morning between two and three a.m. on his way to work.

"At first I thought it was a very large coyote," Rob told me. "I was driving down (Township Route) P in mid-February when I saw something in the ditch. As I approached, it stood up! I've never seen a coyote do that. It stared at me and watched as I drove past."

A few nights later Rob saw what looked like the same creature at the intersection of Township Routes P and Z. First, he noticed yellow eyes in the ditch, and then a large canine creature walked out and crossed the road on all fours, totally unafraid.

He saw it again on April 25, standing on two feet.

He described the creatures as resembling my drawing of "the indigenous dogman."

"From nose to rump it is about five feet long," he said, "and weighs an easy 100 pounds. It's grey in color, the head shape is long with a pointy nose. I've seen dogs on two legs but not comfortably standing there. I had to stop the car and he didn't care. Its fur was long and wild, unkempt, and unclean. Its long and bushy tail was about eighteen inches.

"It had an arch in its back, so it stood hunched over—and a very skinny waist. When he stood up his hands were not in a position like begging for something…but he stood up like a human would with arms to his sides but not all the way back.

"I'm probably the most serious person around," he added, confirming what his sister told me.

I was able to prowl that sighting area myself at the same time of night very soon after his last sighting. My friend Kim Del Rio borrowed a video camera equipped for night photos and we drove around the area for hours but saw only a deer and a fox.

The adventure did demonstrate how difficult it is to get a photo of something at night from a moving car, however. Kim tried to film the fox and deer as I slowed up—she was riding with the video camera already aimed out the open window—but neither creature showed up on the camera.

Powers Lake, by the way, sits about midway between a chain of lakes that starts with Lauderdale in northern Walworth County and

Muddy creek that crosses Bray Road

179

stretches southeast into Kenosha County and northeastern Illinois. Again, waterways seem to be a key sightings element. Bray Road may have been simply a handy place to stop along the feeding trail between them.

Manitoba Monster

Before I close the sightings portion of this book, I want to mention that I do get occasional reports from other countries. I have one from Canada that was simply too interesting to leave out.

A woman wrote to me in April, 2009, that in 1986 she had an encounter in Northern Manitoba that seemed similar to many in my books. She wrote:

"I was spending the night at a friend's house when she went into the kitchen to get a glass of water. A second later, she started screaming that there was something in the front yard looking into the house. I ran to the kitchen to see what the problem was.

"At the front of the house there was a large bay window. If you looked through the doorway from the kitchen and through the living room, you could see the street. Anyway, under the street lamp was this large wolf-like animal standing on its hind legs, staring into the house.

"As I started walking toward the bay window, it crossed the front lawn toward the house, walking on its hind legs. As it walked, I saw that it had the hind legs of a wolf. It was five or six feet tall, had the head and face of a wolf, but its shoulders and arms were like a man's. It was dark grey in colour, with a coarse, shaggy fur.

"It got about as far as the front sidewalk when my friend turned on the outside light. That scared it off. The encounter lasted less than a minute, but I did get a good look at it. I also felt that it had no intention of hurting anyone.

"The next morning, when I left to go home, I saw paw prints in the snow. Its paws were bigger than my hand. Keep in mind that it walked upright on legs similar to the hind legs of a wolf. My friend refused to go anywhere by herself for weeks after that."

This story is another illustration of the many spooky observations of the upright wolf's apparent fascination with human houses. I am not sure what to make of it, since manwolves do not seem to rip their way into windows or screen doors to get at food like bears, but it is creepy to contemplate.

This encounter also has that eerie quality somewhere between *National Geographic* and *The Twilight Zone* that keeps me perpetually pondering the upright manwolf's true essence. I'll offer some parting thoughts on that in the next and final section.

PART FIVE

Nature of the Beast

Some eighteen years and many, many reports after the first Beast of Bray Road story broke, it would be logical to assume that I'd have a much better handle on what this prowling, upright creature might actually be. It would be logical, yes, but untrue. Instead, I have discovered a growing profusion of theories that range from mundane to outrageous—and no clear winner among them.

I cannot declare the manwolf or dogman is *definitely* one thing or another because there still has been no live or dead capture and no irrefutable photo or video to examine. There are some footprints, such as those I found between Milwaukee and Racine, but these vary from site to site in odd ways and are also subject to change and interference from weather and other prints. Photos and videos purporting to show a dogman usually reveal no more than a blurry shadow, a digitally altered image or someone in a costume.

Those folks who are sure they know what the creature is—or is not—may have better information than I do, or perhaps are they simply more willing to skate on really thin evidential ice. I have been told that the creature is *definitely* supernatural, *definitely* a natural wolf, *definitely* a misidentified bear, and *definitely* many other things by equally ardent and intelligent people, all of whom are very welcome to form their own opinions. That is exactly what I urge readers to do. But while do I have my pet theories that I cosset and feed little meat cookies, I just cannot go to that land of all-knowingness yet.

The Beast of Bray Road and *Hunting the American Werewolf* cover the most of the possible origins I've found so far, but I'll give some top contenders another quick go. And I have a queasy feeling as I look at the list, that the official directions for this creature-puzzle should probably state, "Check some, none, or all of the above, as they may be equally true."

Chapter 24

Transformers

Back in 1994, only two years after my Bray Road story broke in *The Week*, I picked up a copy of *Fangoria*, the premiere magazine devoted to monster, horror and sci-fi films, and was amused to learn it was their all-werewolf edition. I bought it and put it on the shelf with my other souvenirs.

During a recent cleaning of that shelf, I found the magazine and decided to actually read the cover story on *Wolf*, Columbia Pictures' film starring Jack Nicholson. I was surprised to learn from journalist Chuck Crisafulli that the movie's screenplay about werewolf transformation was based on screenwriter Jim Harrison's own experience.

It happened in the early 1980s, Harrison said, while he was at a cabin in some remote area of Michigan—interesting, given Michigan's large number of creature sightings. Harrison was apparently experiencing some severe stress in his life at the time and was staying there alone.

He heard wolves howling for several nights after seeing one in the nearby forest, and was having a difficult time getting to sleep one evening when he saw a sudden flash of light from some unknown source—possibly auto headlights. The light caused him to jump out of bed so forcefully that he hit his head on a deer antler chandelier, and next thing he knew he was ripping the cabin's door off its hinges.

All of that could be explained by a combination of adrenaline and emotional distress. However, Harrison said he then realized that he had grown hair all over his face. "I was Lon Chaney, Jr. for a few minutes," he said in the article. The shock of that discovery evidently brought him out of his budding transformation, and he sat outside quietly until the episode had passed and the fur-face receded.

The lupine makeover did not happen again, and Harrison seemed relieved, adding that "a werewolf transformation is something you only want to go through once in your life."

Zounds! And here I've been saying for eighteen years that I don't believe Hollywood-style, flesh-and-bone physical transformations from human to animal are possible or even probable.

I still say that. If true traditional werewolves *were* possible, they'd be all over YouTube by now. As for Harrison, I think that someone in a hypnopompic state of semi-sleep might very well hallucinate something like the feel of fur on the skin, and that this feeling would naturally fade as the person awoke.

Crisafulli, though, said that Harrison was impressed enough to ask several veterinarians what physical changes would be necessary for a human to fully change into a wolf besides the obvious fur and a complete skeletal re-build. The answers were fascinating: The stomach would have to super-size itself to hold the quantity of meat that a wolf is able to eat, the structure and muscles of the jaw would have to ramp up considerably in order to crunch bone, and all the joints would have to grow cushier pads to accommodate leaping. I'm sure countless other changes would be required, including the sticky question of whether a person's DNA would have to transmute in order to override one set of genetic characteristics for another.

DNA, after all, is the set of instructions that tells our genes what to do—or what not to do. As mammals of about the same size, humans and wolves probably share a lot of identical DNA, but there are some fairly drastic and obvious differences between our two species that might prove hard to reconcile.

If one living species is changing into another living species, wouldn't the genetic instructions have to change first in order for that to happen? You could not very well have round pink ears morphing into big pointy hairy ears as long as the DNA for pink round ears remained in charge.

But what if the DNA could somehow change? We do know that some genes can be "switched" on and off by certain conditions. It just seems to me—and of course this is pure speculation—that if a full-grown human body's genetic sequences all changed at once, the result might be horrible death rather than euphoric physical transformation as the physical cells struggled to catch up or died in shock from the mismatch.

It is true that scientists have created chimeras, or living beings whose bodies contain DNA from two distinct species, in the laboratory from two closely related animals such as fish, but these were done at an embryonic stage and resulted in a creature with *shared* characteristics. So far as I know, science has yet to prove that an adult of one species can be wholly and physically transmogrified into another.

Not everyone believes the morphing process occurs at body level. There are people who feel their transformations into wolves are real—but spiritual rather than physical. I certainly do not dispute that people could have such feelings and that such folk may identify very strongly with wolves. I hear from some of them now and then. They may call themselves Therianthropes or Therians, although I have also encountered some members of this group who go by the terms Lycanthropes or Lycans even though these names usually denote full-body changers. It can get confusing. To document all the claims and permutations of every lupine-focused group would take another book.

The movement seems to be growing as werewolves become ever more common in popular media. For instance, when I receive emails from self-declared werewolves using terms like "Crinos" to describe the "upright form," I know someone has been role-playing *Werewolf: The Apocalypse*.

What I tell people who write me is that I don't believe the creatures I research are human at all, and that my studies probably have very little to do with them. They usually reply, "Oh. Carry on, then."

In the meantime, I'm still waiting for that first confirmed transformational video.

Historical Dogmen

Although I have used the terms "dogman" and "manwolf" almost interchangeably in this book—excusable, I think, since no one really knows for sure what these upright canids are—the idea of dogmen has deep roots in human culture and religion. And the traits of dogmen are often quite different than those of the traditional werewolf.

Perhaps because dogs are so close to people socially, dogmen have historically been conceived of as odd humans with canine heads, or *cynocephali*, rather than raging beasts. They may be wholly natural creatures, and some have maintained societies with arts like metalsmithing that require fingers, according to early writers such as the Roman historian Pliny the Elder or 13th Century explorer Marco Polo (touched on briefly in Chapter 7).

Polo also noted that while *cynocephali* were not above grilling up some people-burgers, they were not widely feared as bloody marauders, as werewolves were in medieval Europe. They were considered to be more like a weird tribe of humans (in Polo's times known as one of the "fabulous races") able even to be converted to Christianity. The patron saint of travelers, St. Christopher, was in fact a dog-headed man named Reprobus, according to one legend.

I don't think that anyone should take Polo's travel diaries as proof that canine-human forms have actually existed in nature, however. Most of these reports were secondhand and may also have been based on the observance of ritual body modifications such as ears or lips enlarged by inserting metal disks. The stories were much-repeated—probably making it easier for people to believe in the scarier werewolves which ate their humans raw and would never qualify for sainthood.

Exceptions to this idea of fully integrated dog-headed humans, however, exist. I found one example in the story culture of the Hopi people of the southwestern U.S. In the fascinating book *The Fourth World of the Hopi*, author Harold Courlander reveals a clan of "dog people" who appear as normal humans when first approached, but which later revert to dog form by donning canine pelts. This method is identical to the transformation rituals described in many historic Scandinavian and European accounts of werewolfery. And that leads us into my next line of inquiry.

Conjured Creatures

I know from my mail that many people are curious whether spirit entities that look like werewolves can be "conjured" into existence by means such as meditative practices, rituals of black magic and shamanic ceremonies (such as wearing animal skins like the Hopi dog people), or by using certain psychotropic drugs. There has been a special interest in persistent rumors that dark rituals were used to produce the creatures seen on Bray Road, but as these allegations are impossible to prove and lack firsthand eyewitness reports, I have not pursued them and have no plan to do so.

If Bray Road were the only location in the country where upright canines have been sighted, then I might consider this scenario a bit more likely. But given the widespread reports of these creatures—and assuming it is possible to "raise" cryptid beasts this way—it seems doubtful there would be so many occultists adept at manifesting demonic werewolves from sea to *The Shining* sea. Still, researchers Janet and Colin Bord give a lot of credence to this possibility in their book, *Alien Animals*, especially in regard to Loch Ness and its monster. And I can't rule it out in all cases.

The idea that humans-plus-magic equals impossible creatures is old and cross-cultural.

Ancient Druid ritual transformation into wolf.
Interpretation by Nathan Godfrey.
Originally created for *MonsterQuest*, "American Werewolf" episode.

In addition to the Hopi story above, I've discussed the Native American phenomena of skinwalkers, skinchangers and bearwalkers at length in other books and in this one (see Chapter 6). These are entities created by magic ritual that look like animals but are really spirit doubles of the shaman that either go out from the physical body or envelope it like a supernatural costume. They are related to the Tibetan idea of *tulpas*, materialized thought-form creatures produced by intense and specific meditative practices, but are usually associated with malicious intent and may be sent to harm or harass a victim. (The idea in Chapter 7 that Oklahoman skinwalkers were short, evil forest creatures was probably not correct and was questioned even by its writer.)

I can tell you that Native Americans from various locations have indicated to me that these things absolutely exist, as do zoomorphic (animal-shaped) spirit guardians made to watch over sacred grounds. In *Hunting the American Werewolf,* I noted my discovery that the main concentrations of ancient Native American burial mounds shaped like traditional "water panthers" were located in almost exactly the same sites as manwolf hotspots. That is certainly an eerie connection that seems to go beyond mere coincidence, but we have no way of knowing what the association truly is. It may be nothing more than the fact that these mounds were usually placed near a lake or river, and that wolves also like well-watered habitats for their own liquid needs and for attracting prey. And yet these associations surface again and again.

A woman of part-Choctaw ancestry wrote in 2009 to tell me of experiences she had growing up in southern Louisiana in a rural area between Rosepine and Leesville, near what looked like a man-made mound that she described as "almost a balcony of dirt."

While digging a garden one year, she and her family unearthed a trove of Native American artifacts: arrowheads, pottery, and the like. She took some of the items to her room to play with them, and on the third night after doing so was visited by something she called "the shadow doggy."

She woke up suddenly in the night to see a black half-man, half-dog with ears on top of its head standing at the door of her bedroom (very like the visitations in Eau Claire, Wis.). She could not see its eyes but knew it was staring at her, and she screamed until her grandmother came running and the thing disappeared. It returned each of the next three nights, and on the fourth night it moved to the side of her bed and mentally communicated that she should put the artifacts back where she found them. She did so the next day, keeping only one arrowhead, which she still has. She said she still feels "watched," even though she now lives in another state. Another explanation might be that this was a sleep-paralysis hallucination—induced by her guilt over taking the objects—but the experience was very real to her.

Dog Soldiers

More mysterious canine forms, according to some Native American friends, may be found in the legends of the Cheyenne Dog Soldiers. The Dog Soldiers began as a fraternal warrior society that dominated rival groups within the Cheyenne people of the Great Plains in the mid-1860s, but they were probably based on much older traditions. Their trademark battle strategy was to stake themselves to the ground with a long sash to show a commitment to fight to the death. At times, they were believed to transform to dog shape during battle, much as Viking warriors known as *berserkers* were said to do in early Norse sagas.

Although the Dog Soldiers' dominance faded after their people's dispersal to reservations, the tradition was never lost, and Cheyenne Dog Soldiers have fought in all major American wars. Some believe Dog

Soldiers come home from war with the ability to shapeshift, and that they are occasionally seen among us in dog form.

Other Native American acquaintances of mine, most notably from the Wisconsin Ho Chunk (Winnebago), have told me that upright canines and the man-ape we call Bigfoot are both known to their people from antiquity, and they are considered spirit creatures that travel between our world (dimension?) and the next. In this viewpoint, there is no trans-species changing going on, although shamans or witches may separately imitate the ape or canine forms. The creatures require food to maintain their energy while in this realm, but they may re-enter the spirit world through certain windows or portals which may often be found in natural springs.

This paradigm is very close to the view of maverick paranormal researcher and author John Keel (best known for his writings on West Virginia's Mothman) who, as noted earlier, held that sightings flap locations might be called "window areas" where things can squeeze through the cracks between dimensions.

I did notice one other otherworldly coincidence as I examined sighting after sighting for this book: The circumstances of many U.S. man-wolf reports bear a striking resemblance to tales of some ancient denizens of Great Britain—black phantom dogs.

Chapter 25

Creatures from Beyond: Hellhound vs. Manwolf

A Wisconsin musician named Scott told me of a black dog-infested place on Okauchee Lake in Waukesha County where he used to spend summers at an aunt's cottage. One of his aunts who also stayed there often held séances and claimed the place was haunted by his great-grandfather, Bernard (no relation to St. Bernards).

Not far from the cottage was a small island where the burned ruins of an old mansion peeked from behind overgrown foliage. The island, said his aunt, could not be approached after dark because of its guardians—large, black, blaze-eyed dogs that patrolled the island on two legs. This was common knowledge among the locals, Scott said, many of whom claimed to have heard the dogs howling.

I discovered that Okauchee Lake has several small islands. A small, occupied island on the east shore lies just north of a vacant island known as Party Island for its traditional boating get-togethers. On the northwest side of the lake is McDowell Island, nicknamed Crazyman's Island! The western shore of the lake was also the site of an ancient, thirty-foot diameter conical Native American burial mound that was reported to historian C.E. Brown in 1907, as well as a linear effigy mound and other mounds and burial sites. Along this western shore lay the tiny isle—referred to by Scott's family as Haunted Island.

Okauchee Lake is part of the Oconomowoc chain of lakes and not far from Waukesha's famous old springs which were sacred to and well-used by the indigenous people, as evidenced by old and much-worn trails found by settlers.

Another American black dog showed up in Palo Duro Canyon State Park near Amarillo, Texas, according to author Nick Redfern in his 2008 book, *There's Something in the Woods*. A woman, her daughter, and son-in-law had gone there for a picnic, said Redfern, when they encountered a huge, aggressive, dark-furred dog much larger than a German shepherd that floated off the ground several times and then disappeared before the family's eyes near a recreated Native American tepee. The canyon's archaeological sites show that humans have lived there for 12,000 years, the most recent being Apache, Comanche and Kiowa.

The elements of these stories and the environmental and historic features that anchor them may seem unique to their Wisconsin and Texas locations but are, in fact, surprisingly similar to Old World black dog lore.

Black Dogs Abroad

I've written elsewhere about Charlotte Bronte character Jane Eyre's encounter with what she took for a *gyrtrash* or black phantom dog (BPD). A few of the many colorful names for this historic and widely seen creature of the British Isles include (varying according to location) Black Shuck, Padfoot, Skriker, and Gwyllgi. Although they commonly haunt old manor houses (like the upright hounds of Okauchee Lake), phantom dogs are most often encountered in church yards and grave-yards and along roads, especially at crossroads. They are usually described as larger than a normal dog and black in color, although some are reported as white, gray, and even green (e.g., the *cu sith*, fairy dogs of Scotland). Their eyes often glow a shining crimson, and they are notoriously difficult to shoot or to capture on film.

Other parts of Europe are also infested with canine spirits. For example, there is an old Germanic legend of a large, shapeshifting canine called the *aufhocker* which author Jonathan Maberry describes in his 2006 book *Vampire Universe* as "a hulking brute of a dog that walks on its hind legs."

Is anything beginning to sound familiar?

The vast majority of American manwolves have been sighted along roadsides and intersections, such as in the incident where two twelve-year-olds saw the large dog-like creature on its hind legs near a cross-roads in Michigan (Chapter 2) and many other accounts in this book, including some incidents at on/off ramps (Manwolves of Muskogee, Chapter 6). In this day of interstate highways and multi-lane thorough-fares, exit and entrance ramps are the modern version of crossroads.

Crossroads are also a common black dog hangout in Latin America, according to author Simon Burchell in *Phantom Black Dogs in Latin America* (Heart of Albion, 2007). He tells of a nineteen-year-old Mayan woman who was walking with her sister in Guatemala City one evening when a giant black hound with "burning" eyes showed up at a crossroad and refused to allow them past. The sisters backed away slowly until the "dog" changed into a white floating blob that followed them. They did not remember the rest of their walk home. This was clearly not a natu-ral animal.

Burchell came to the same conclusion that I did regarding the sim-ilarity between Old World and New World BPDs. He wrote, "...here we have a Black Dog appearing to a modern Maya girl in a way that close-ly parallels historical accounts from Britain such as the account from Uplyme in 1856 of a Black Dog that seemed to 'swell into a cloud' before vanishing into thin air…"

The trans-Atlantic parallel holds in other ways, too.

Grave Consequences

Graveyards—both new and ancient—and other sacred spaces such as ancient burial mounds and effigy sites are another type of locale that manwolves and BPDs often have in common in Europe and the Americas. In England, the BPDs seen around holy grounds are called church grims or grimes. The "grime" part refers to their dark or grimey color. In the Americas, they are more likely to be called hellhounds or devil dogs. But they look and act much the same. You may recall the Oklahoma hound that sat on the church sign in Chapter 6.

In addition to some of the dogman stories cited in this book, I found an older New England account from the late 1880s of a *loup-garou*, French for werewolf, which was very like a BPD in looks and behavior. Author B.A. Botkin retold a story in *A Treasury of New England Folklore* (Crown, 1965) of creatures that changed from men to black dogs or wolves to haunt graveyards and roads.

The original story came from an 1894 book called *Danvis Folks* by Rowland E. Robinson. A man of French descent reported that he had set out one winter evening to fetch a priest to give his dying father last rites. He was near the priest's home (and presumably the church) when behind him on the road he saw a "beeg, beeg black dawg" following him on its hind legs. The creature ran to the man and put its forepaws on his shoulders while the man tried to grab for his knife. Local lore held that drawing the blood of a *loup-garou* would force it to change back to human. Unable to draw his blade, the man could smell the creature's fetid breath and feel the brush of its fur—and had given himself up for dead when the priest came running and yelled a rebuke that made the creature run away into the woods.

For comparison's sake, I'll mention just a few of the more recent cemetery incidents here, such as the 1994 sighting of a dark, upright canine near the cemetery at Chicago's Great Lakes Naval Base by three guards, Rick Renzulli's run-in with two oversized quadrupeds near a Kenosha, Wis. cemetery in 1984 (both examples from *Hunting*), and the summer, 2000 sighting near Michigan's Fort Custer Recreation Area cemetery cited in Chapter 4 of this book. None of them involved such a narrow escape as the French man's, but they left equally deep impressions on the witnesses.

Dogs and other bone-scavenging canines have long been associated with graveyards and the dead, going back to prehistoric times in all parts of the world, so it is not hard to see where the original notion of cemetery ghost hounds came from. But why, when people have for centuries buried the dead in boxes six feet under the soil, would anyone still see predatory phantom pooches in these areas?

Good Vibrations

I wonder whether the connection between canines and church cemeteries has more to do with the characteristics of the cemetery sites than with the presence of corpses. Most churches in Great Britain were built upon ancient places of pagan worship, which, as in ancient America, were often selected for geographical features such as height of the land, proximity to water (especially springs) and rock formations. Incidentally, high land with water access also makes for an ideal military fort or camp, another type of sighting locale that pops up more and more frequently in my reports.

To borrow a theory often put forth by paranormal researchers to explain the presence of human ghosts, perhaps these sites hold thousands of years-worth of psychokinetic energy—a very hard-to-define substance—from all the emotional drama that has played out in them over the centuries, and this holdover energy manifests in the shape of man's best friend. It makes some sense if you can accept the idea that energy from living creatures not only persists in the atmosphere but retains enough strength to show up for many years. It seems a farfetched theory but perhaps is possible through some process not yet known at our present level of science. (Of course, almost *any*thing is possible though some process not yet known to science.)

Or—still on the very speculative side—it may be that this type of site contains minerals such as quartz that emit energy due to pressure from the slow movements of surfaces beneath the ground. This type of energy is called piezoelectricity, although whether it can result from subterranean activity or not is controversial. But some researchers have theorized that these same underground movements could also produce very low sound waves that the human brain translates into particular animal forms.

That is not so far-fetched, bizarre as it seems. A 1998 British experiment (article "The Ghost in the Machine," Vic Tandy) has shown that sound waves at a particular low frequency—19 Hertz—can induce visions of spectral figures. Any sound below the normal human hearing range of 20 Hertz is called infrasound, which can also be produced by large mammals such as tigers, elephants, and, say some, Bigfoot. Other experiments have shown that certain frequencies of infrasound can also produce feelings of dread and fear and symptoms such as chills or nausea, all common features of encounters with cryptids.

Ley Lines and Water

Another similarity between Old and New World mystery hounds: the Bords in *Alien Animals* note that most BPD sightings occur very near water, something that shows up in nearly every American beast sighting, as well. Even Bray Road has a small creek trickling through part of it.

The Bords have also have documented the fact that in Great Britain, BPDs often appear on or near ley lines, which are commonly defined as an invisible grid of energy lines emanating from the earth that connect locations of many sacred sites. In Great Britain, they may be visibly observed as straight "tracks" or ancient footpaths worn into the soil between churches and ancient stone monuments.

But what about ley lines in the United States? Methods of determining their location vary from dowsing to simply connecting ancient centers, so it's hard to say exactly where they lie although there are a few maps floating around the Internet. I was intrigued, however, by a book called *The Atlantis Blueprint* (by Colin Wilson and Rand Flem-Ath) that argues the world's great sacred monuments—especially ancient pyramids—are located along certain numerically related degrees of longitude and latitude. This is *not* the same thing as ley lines. Longitude and latitude are human inventions by which we map and measure the globe, not inherent tracks of "earth current." Wilson and Flem-Ath contend that the placement of ancient sites along latitude and longitude implies an ancient civilization with geographical and astronomical knowledge that was advanced enough to correctly determine longitude and latitude.

Just for fun I looked up the coordinates for Wisconsin's ancient Mississippian pyramids at Aztalan, for Bray Road, and for the Yucatan's great Mayan center of Chichen-Itza with its ancient astronomical observatory. The longitudes are 88.85, 88.52, and 88.34 west respectively, all between only half a degree away from 88! However, to play my own spoilsport, there are lots of other sighting hotspots *not* at 88 degrees— and probably also lots of them that would line up with other cool ancient places.

To play with latitudes, Aztalan, Big Rapids, Michigan (Dogman hotspot), and La Crosse, Wisconsin (Manbat, lizard man) are all just a few minutes over 43 degrees north.

The creature-as-geocache treasure still does not quite work for me, though. While a hypothetical, ancient, inexplicably sky-faring culture may have had some personal reason to teach people from the Mayans to the Mississippians how to line their major centers up by certain longitudes, why (and how) would they have thrown a pile of werewolves onto Bray Road in between?

I was still surprised that these off-the-cuff picks seemed to line up so neatly. I don't know if the numbers have any significance in themselves, but suspect I could find many such correlations between sighting hotspots and sacred sites if I devoted enough time to the task.

Meaningful or not, there appears to be a strange entanglement between BPDs, manwolves and their habitats and haunts. Perhaps that is another confirmation that we are looking at a world-wide phenomenon and not just at isolated oddities. It also helps open up the possibility that appearances of BPDs and manwolves may be triggered somehow by sound and by electromagnetic properties of the earth itself. I recommend Paul Devereaux's *Haunted Land* and Persinger and Lafreniere's *Space-Time Transients and Unusual Events* for further reading on the complex connection between strange creature sighting and geological features.

There are still some differences between manwolves and BPDs. The red eye color seen in British encounters is at odds with most American reports, although the scarlet gaze shows up in the U.S. from time to time. And most phantom dogs of the British Isles remain on all fours rather than prancing on two feet. But I think the similarities between these weird canine entities are far too enticing to ignore.

Timewalkers

One more way British and American unknown canines are alike is their seeming ability to melt away at whim. An idea proposed by writer Gordon Stein in *FATE* magazine (June, 1990), is that "the black dog of British folklore seems to live outside of the concept of human time. It appears and disappears from human sight by its own contrivance."

That struck a chord with me, especially the last line. An extremely consistent feature of manwolf reports is that the creature comes and goes on its own terms. Even when surprised by a traveler at its roadside dinner, it makes its escape easily—often after making a quick lunge to scare or distract the witness.

The late Robert Beutlich, a Chicago engineer who was an officer and practitioner of Radionics (using electronics to "tune in" to other dimensions), also put forth the theory in *Hunting* that these seemingly out-of-place creatures are instead out-of-time creatures.

"Time dislocation zones are part of the earth grid that is run off the pyramids," said Beutlich (echoing the theme of Wilson and Flem-Ath). "There are pyramids all over the world…and the time dislocation zones are also the teleportation zones."

Beutlich's view dovetails neatly with the Native American idea of "spirit creatures" that know where and how to teleport. It would also explain why some sightings resemble long-gone species such as dire wolves or even killer kangaroos (see below).

But if the past is truly able to leak dire wolves—which show no skeletal sign of having been bipedal—then by rights we should also be getting reports of T. rexes, saber-toothed tigers, giant ground sloths, and a whole exotic panorama of extinct fauna rather than just the occasional pteranodon or highly developed man-ape. While it's true that some wildly odd creatures are sighted around the globe, the sightings fall far short a fair representation of all the species that existed back in the day. Perhaps if time dislocations do happen, the portals are run by some mighty selective gatekeepers. Or maybe some critters know how to pick the locks.

Chapter 26

Bone and Blood

The Bear Facts

It's weird, I know. I never have nightmares about manwolves, but I admit to having a life-long phobia about bears. It's probably because I spent many childhood vacations in bear-abundant Price County, and I've seen more than one in the wild. That is not the reason, however, that I have been interested in the amazing number of bear sightings from Madison to Milwaukee and up the Lake Michigan shore in late spring and early summer of 2010. Bears have been invading backyards and bird feeders as far south as Verona in Dane County.

Not only does it make me wonder if a lumbering bruin will show up in my own "hood"—we had a cougar very near here a few years ago —it brings all kinds of comparisons with manwolf sightings to mind.

Skeptics very commonly dismiss most manwolf sightings as wrongly-identified bears, even when the physical descriptions are very different (e.g., bears walk flat-footed and have bulky lower bodies; canines walk on toepads and are slender in hip area, etc.).

If bears really were the basis for most cryptid canine sightings, however, then manwolf reports should have shot through the roof during that time, with lots of people misidentifying all those bears. In fact, the opposite was true. Reports of crypto-critters trickled to a near-stop. The fact is most people know a bear when they see one and can easily distinguish it from other animals.

The other aspect that fascinated me in these recent bear sightings is that the nomadic bears all starred in photographs or videos on the evening news. Bears are not elusive nor do they seem camera-shy. They also don't fake-attack and run in these videos—especially not on their hind legs—as do most reported manwolves. And I have yet to see even one convincing photo—let alone video—of a purported manwolf.

The two styles of behavior are strikingly different.

Why is that? Is it greater elusiveness on the part of the manwolves? Nocturnal habits that make manwolves less likely to be spotted? A carnivore's disinterest in birdfeeders and garbage cans that sit near houses within easy camera range?

Or is there some slightly world-beyond aspect to the manwolf that makes it (and Bigfoot) unphotographable? It is almost as if they are just a click out of sync with what we and our cameras are physically equipped to perceive. There are just as many witnesses of upright unknown canids as there are of recent bear sightings, yet we don't have the photographic goods to prove it.

And there lies the ongoing rub.

Killer Marsupials

Another natural animal often cited as a possible stand-in for supposed manwolves is the kangaroo. 'Roos do have upright ears and a long face with muzzle, and they get around in an upright position, although they hop rather than run. And although they are not native to North America, Wisconsin and other states have had a surprising number of kangaroo sighting flaps. One of the earliest happened in June, 1899 in New Richmond, Wisconsin, on the state's western border in St. Croix County, when a Mrs. Glover was astonished to see a kangaroo pass through her neighbor's backyard. (There is a Glover Park in New Richmond and a home called the Ezra Glover House is on the National Register of Historic Places.)

Coon Rapids, Minnesota, which lies west of New Richmond across the Mississippi River, hosted a decade-long rash of kangaroo sightings from 1957 to 1967, and in 1974 both Illinois and Wisconsin experienced kangaroo flaps from Chicago to Waukesha, where one witness produced a blurry and therefore disputable photo. Eyewitnesses also reported 'roos in North Carolina in 1981 and 1987.

Most of these cases are never solved—circus and exotic pet escapees are almost always ruled out—nor are the mysterious animals captured, except for one out-of-place red 'roo seen bounding around southwestern Wisconsin in January, 2005, that was caught near Dodgeville and now resides in Madison's Vilas Park Zoo. He is called

Boomer, and while his origin has never been discovered, he is assuredly not a phantom.

To my knowledge, his presence in western Wisconsin did not spark any dogman reports, either.

That doesn't surprise me; I don't think that modern kangaroos much resemble werewolves. But their ancestors may have. In July, 2006, a *National Geographic* news article by Sean Markey announced that a team of Australian archaeologists had discovered the dog-sized fossil of what they dubbed a "killer kangaroo." Officially named Ekaltadeta, it had wolf-like fangs, big forelimbs, and galloped rather than hopped. Its jaws and teeth were designed to rip through bone and flesh.

These fearsome creatures, however, lived in what is now Australia around twenty million years ago, so an appearance of one in modern times would be about twenty million times less likely than an appearance of a modern kangaroo. That is, unless, time portal leaks do exist.

Bigfoot, Baboons and Buffoons

Another staple question I'm asked in almost every interview is whether the unknown canines might really be unknown apes. By that, the questioner usually means Bigfoot, but baboons have been brought up, too. I dealt at greater length with baboons in Chapter 8, "Texas Terribles." They may have somewhat dog-like heads but do not walk

upright, and they are flat-footed. Bigfoots walk upright but have a man-like skeletal structure, no pointed ears on top of the head, no long muzzle, no tail, and do not walk on clawed toe pads.

In both cases, canine and primate physical structure and movements are so different that witnesses who have a good look at a dogman or Bigfoot are usually pretty sure of what they saw. Foot prints are especially different between the two.

Bigfoots and manwolves do sometimes occupy the same or adjacent territories. While Elkhorn and areas east and south of it in Wisconsin are famous for manwolf sightings, most of the reports starting about ten miles north of Elkhorn, and just to the north and west, feature definite Bigfoots. Besides others detailed in my first two books, there have been two sightings from credible witnesses near the Lima Marsh in 2005, and another came in just as I was proofreading the manuscript for this book.

Lima Marsh, area near Bigfoot sightings

It occurred earlier, around 1999, halfway between Elkhorn and Whitewater, near North Lake and only a scant twelve miles from Lima Center. A Chicago computer salesman named Joe was on his way to fish at the lake one day and was about a mile north of Millard on County Hwy O when he noticed movement on the east side of the road through his passenger window.

He slowed down and saw a seven-foot, 400-pound creature walking through the tall grass in the ditch, swinging its long arms from big shoulders and leaning slightly forward as if intent on where it was going. It was covered in "rust brown" fur that appeared uneven and unkempt, and as it turned its head to look at him, Joe said his first thought was, "Whoa, that is not a person!"

His second thought was, "Don't stop the car."

The creature's eyes were "sunken into" the fur that covered its face, he said, and no ears or muzzle were visible. He said it reminded him of Chewbacca from *Star Wars*. He kept on driving and did not look back— and never told anyone about it. He is not into the supernatural at all, he said, but he came across my *Beast of Bray Road* site while browsing the Internet only a few days earlier and, because that was in Elkhorn too, assumed he had seen the Beast. But when I asked him to describe what he saw, his answer made it clear this was no canine.

Here is a list of other sightings within about a twenty-mile radius of that area:

- 1964 – Man sees "Bigfoot creature" cross road and hurdle fence northwest of Delavan.

- 1970s – Two women, a group of campers separately see Bigfoot-like "Bluff Monster" between Elkhorn and Palmyra.

- 1972 – Jefferson County creature described like Bigfoot by woman slashes horse on farm.

- 1980 – Bipedal, hairy hominoid encountered north of Whitewater on Bark Rd. by Ronald Nixon.

- 1993 – Andrew Hurd sees Bigfoot in family's barn near Hebron.

- 1994 – David and Mary Pagliaroni see Bigfoot 10 feet from car at Honey Creek bridge.

- 1999 – Joe sees Bigfoot on Cty O just north of Millard (above).

- 2005, March – UW-Whitewater student sees probable Bigfoot cross Hwy 59 near Lima Marsh.

- 2005, April – Business owners Lenny and Stacy Faytus see Bigfoot at dusk near Lima Marsh.

- 2005, September 16 – Young man sees possible juvenile Bigfoot at Cty B & White Pigeon Rd., Bloomfield Township, Walworth County.

- 2010, July 15 – A Jefferson County woman saw a six-to-seven-foot-tall creature covered in dark fur with long arms swinging at his sides and "gorilla-like legs" enter the treeline on the south side of State Hwy 106 at Jaeckel Rd. at 4:00 p.m.—she pulled right over, but the creature had disappeared from view.

Both the Pagliaronis and the Bloomfield man passed rigorous polygraphs administered by an expert hired by the *MonsterQuest* producers. It seems like a fairly impressive list, given the time span of about four decades and the rather small geographical area. The witness descriptions all describe something seven to eight feet tall, fur-covered, man-like in shape but with longer arms, no visible ears or protruding muzzle, and totally upright. Crazed Bigfoot hunts have been conducted in other places on far less witness testimony.

I think if there is a Bigfoot population here, then it must be rather small or consist of roamers from other places. It is interesting that the southern unit of the Kettle Moraine State Forest seems to be a rough dividing line between Bigfoot and Manwolf sightings, with most of the former west and south and the latter east and south. I imagine they eat nearly the same prey.

If Bigfoots and manwolves really are natural animals competing for virtually the same food, then this territorial division is completely necessary and expected. If they are inter-dimensional beings erupting now and then from watery portals, they still might not want to mix. But the fact that both cryptids are present within such a small area may be an important part of the puzzle.

As for the buffoon—hoaxers—part of the above subtitle, I think it's evident from the many incidents cited in this book and my previous two that there is no way human pranks could account for more than a miniscule number of sightings. The sightings are simply too widespread and are often in places too remote for someone to go to that much trouble.

Most telling, though, is the fact that no hoaxes I've looked at have matched up with any reported sightings to serve as explanations for them.

Author interpretation of most witness descriptions of Bigfoot

Wolves

The most obvious and plausible animal that might serve as a natural basis for sightings is the increasingly common Eastern grey, or timber, wolf. A report from Wisconsin's Department of Natural Resources in June, 2010 affirmed that the state's wolf population was up a whopping ten percent in the past year alone. Like black bears and cougars, wolves have recently shown their muzzled faces in areas of the state unaccustomed to large, wild predators. And, as shown earlier, at least two observers of large quadrupeds on Bray Road insist that they saw grey wolves and nothing else.

That may well be, but if it is true, then some grey wolves have learned to walk around on two legs when the mood takes them. Many sober, serious witnesses have also seen them in bipedal mode. It is not an impossible adaptation, and studies have shown wolves are intelligent enough to teach helpful behaviors to their young.

Moreover, I can see many advantages to such a posture, especially in Midwestern states once composed of large tracts of prairie grasses and now featuring large tracts of cornfields. By walking upright, a wolf could see over the grass to look for deer or bison. It could carry away chunks of meat in its forelimbs (as many manwolves have been observed to do) rather than having to drag it with its mouth, a much more vulnerable position. It could walk through mud or swamps and get only two paws wet rather than four, and it would have an optional position to use when trying to stay unseen in any environment.

Mounted Eastern grey timber wolf on display at Blue Island Public Library, Blue Island, Illinois

The process of natural selection is well known and could be easily applied here. The wolves most successful at maintaining an upright posture would likely be those with the largest paws, for balance and for holding things. They would teach the behavior to their offspring and natural selection would gradually create a group of upright, long-pawed wolves. Their intelligence might also be enhanced as the freed-up forelimbs performed new behaviors, and probably only the more intelligent wolves would remain elusive enough to hide their behavior. The final result is the creature I call the Indigenous Dogman. But while it would explain many of the manwolf's puzzling behaviors, I still have not found any indication from those who study grey wolves that wild wolves are the slightest bit inclined to get up and boogie.

Perhaps the researchers are simply not studying the right wolves.

A Final Word

I wish that this book could erupt in a big hosanna moment right now, with fireworks and Major Announcements to the World. I wish. It would make for a much better ending. But, as I said earlier in this section, I can honestly only continue to make my best guess at the truth on a case by case basis.

And in the final tally, I think that only a tiny fraction of sightings may be due to hoaxers and another very small percentage to misidentification of various species of natural animals or to visual misperceptions. Most reports of upright wolves or dogs, in my opinion, describe either natural canines that have learned or evolved an optional bipedal posture, or mysterious canine look-alike entities born of forces that we little understand.

I rather hope it is the former.

Linda S. Godfrey

Author and artist Linda Godfrey is a former teacher and newspaper reporter who became a leading authority on modern-day unknown canines—or werewolves—after breaking the story *The Beast of Bray Road* in 1992. Besides a book by that title, she has also written *Hunting the American Werewolf* (basis of the History Channel show *MonsterQuest's* first episode), three books in the Chelsea House *Mysteries, Legends and Unexplained* series (*Werewolves, Lake and Sea Monsters*, and *Mythical Creatures*), *Weird Michigan, Strange Wisconsin, The Poison Widow, Haunted Wisconsin: Ghosts and Strange Phenomena in the Badger State,* and (co-authored) *Weird Wisconsin* and S*trange Wisconsin.* She has appeared on many national TV and radio shows, such as Travel Channel, *Inside Edition*, the *New In Search Of, America's Scariest Places*, *National* and *Wisconsin Public Radio, Coast to Coast AM,* and more. She lives in Wisconsin with her husband and their monstrous dog, Grendel.

She maintains web sites at www.beastofbrayroad.com and www.weirdmichigan.com.

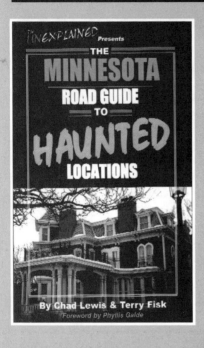

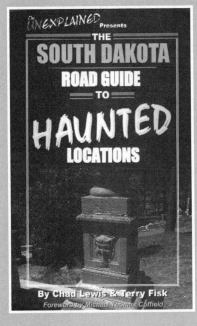

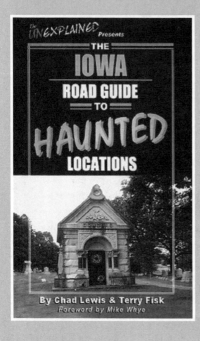

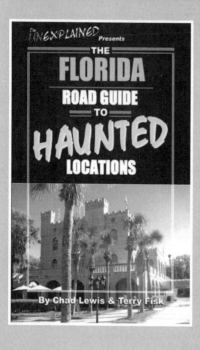

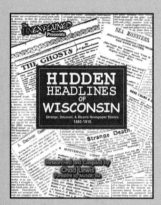
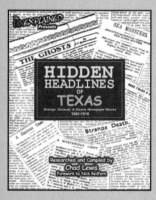

"The Unexplained" Sweatshirt

COLOR: Black
SIZES: M, L, XL, 2XL

Hooded. 100% cotton. "The Unexplained with Chad Lewis and Terry Fisk" on front.

"The Unexplained" Tee shirt

COLOR: Black
SIZES: M, L, XL, 2XL

Short-sleeved. 100% cotton. "The Unexplained with Chad Lewis and Terry Fisk" on front.

Unexplained Research LLC
P.O. Box 2173
Eau Claire, WI 54702-2173
www.unexplainedresearch.com
admin@unexplainedresearch.com